Praise for *My Life in a Cat House*

"Cooper, who charmed readers with the best-selling memoir of her intrepid blind cat, *Homer's Odyssey*, returns with escapades of other past and present felines. Cooper's witty, breezy writing, her unabashed love of felines, and her admission that her spoiled cats have trained her will delight and resonate with cat people."
--*Library Journal*

"Fans of *Homer's Odyssey* will rejoice upon hearing that Homer's owner, Cooper, has returned with more true cat stories...both hilarious and deeply moving. Readers...will delight in these anecdotes of cats who seemingly have something to say about everything. Fans of Vicky Myron and Brett Witter's *Dewey* and James Bowen's *A Street Cat Named Bob* will be highly satisfied."
--*Booklist*

"If you've ever lived with a cat, then this book is for you ... In *My Life in a Cat House,* Cooper lovingly and humorously depicts the ups and downs of a life with cats and the ways in which they mimic human behavior and feelings. A fun read for all animal lovers."
—*New York Journal of Books*

"A literary fur fix for Homer fans!"
--*Catster* **magazine**

"As Gwen shares the joys, sorrows, laughter and tears of sharing her life with her cats, both past and present, you will find yourself nodding in recognition and perhaps remember the antics of a cat long gone. You may even gain a deeper understanding of your own feline companions...

Gwen is a brilliant writer who can evoke emotion like no other. Her writing goes straight for the reader's

heart. *My Life in a Cat House* is a treat for the cat lover's soul."
--The Conscious Cat

"Gwen has the uncanny ability to touch our hearts with her gift of conveying thought-provoking and heart-stirring emotions…Gwen's writing is unpretentious, it's authentic, it's REAL. Whether like me you have nearly all of Gwen's books, or if this one is your first, you will delight in her descriptive, often hilarious and loving stories about her cats."
--Cat Chat with Caren and Cody

"There's something about Gwen Cooper's cat books that touch my heart like few others, and *My Life in a Cat House* is no exception. Whether you've enjoyed every one of Gwen's cat books or this is your first, snuggle up with a cat or two while you're reading. I guarantee with each turn of the page you'll pull them just a little bit closer as you realize just how empty your life would be without their unconditional love."
--Melissa's Mochas, Mysteries and Meows

"This book perfectly encapsulates the unique and amazing experience of being owned by cats and the joy they bring into our lives. That alone is reason enough to read it."
—James Bowen, international bestselling author of *A Street Cat Named Bob*

"Gwen Cooper is the Queen of Cat Love—and in these fun and frisky stories, she perfectly captures all the reasons felines rule our hearts and our homes. No cat lover should be without this book, but more important, give it to the

folks who haven't yet seen the light. At least they'll understand us better!"
—**Sy Montgomery, bestselling author of** *How to Be a Good Creature: A Memoir in Thirteen Animals*

"What a pleasure to read [Gwen Cooper's] beautiful stories, brimming with her cat-love and even more important her ability to get you to actually see her cats . . . You will want to see more and more. She can become your next obsession, as she has become mine!"
—**Jeffrey Moussaieff Masson, international bestselling author of** *The Nine Emotional Lives of Cats*

"An elegant, incisive account of love, laughter, and the deep meaning and magic cats add to our lives."
—**Britt Collins, author of** *Strays: A Lost Cat, a Homeless Man, and Their Journey Across America*

Praise for *Homer's Odyssey*

"Touching…one not to miss."
--*USA Today*

"This memoir about adopting a special-needs kitten teaches that sometimes in life, you have to take a blind leap."
--*People*

"Cooper is a genial writer with both a sense of humor and a gift for conveying the inner essence of an animal."
--*The Christian Science Monitor*

"Delightful…This lovely human-feline memoir, following in the footsteps of Vicki Myron's bestselling

Dewey: The Small-Town Library Cat Who Touched the World, is sure to warm the hearts of all pet lovers."
--Library Journal

"A poignant story, well written with...tenderness and realism...Your life will be richer for having taken this journey with [Gwen and Homer]."
--I Love Cats **magazine**

Praise for *Love Saves the Day*

"Prudence [is a] sassy but sensitive feline heroine."
--Time

"Cooper brings readers a...tale that cat lovers will treasure...This book will make most readers laugh and cry, and probably lead them to wonder more often what, exactly, their pet is thinking."
--Fredericksburg *Free Lance-Star*

"Once again Gwen Cooper shines her light on the territory that defines the human/animal bond. In *Love Saves the Day*, she creates an emotional landscape so beautifully complete that we can't help but share in the heartbreaks and triumphs of her characters, regardless of their species. That, in itself, is a reason to stand up and cheer."
--Jackson Galaxy, star of *My Cat From Hell* **and** *New York Times* **bestselling author of** *Total Cat Mojo*

"*Love Saves the Day* eloquently explains why so many of us would do anything at all for our pets."
--Barbara Delinsky, *New York Times* **bestselling author of** *Escape*

Other Cat Books and Stories by Gwen Cooper

*Homer's Odyssey:
A Fearless Feline Tale, or How I Learned
About Love and Life with a Blind Wonder Cat*

Homer: The Ninth Life of a Blind Wonder Cat

*My Life in a Cat House: True Tales of Love, Laughter,
and Living with Five Felines*

Homer and the Holiday Miracle

Love Saves the Day: A Novel

The Curl Up with a Cat Tale Series

SPRAY ANYTHING

*More True Tales About
Homer and the Gang*

GWEN COOPER

Copyright © 2020 by Gwen Cooper
All rights reserved.

Spray Anything: More True Tales About Homer and the Gang
A Curl Up with a Cat Tale Book

Copyright © 2020 by Gwen Cooper
All rights reserved. This book or any portion thereof
may not be reproduced or used in any manner whatsoever
without the express written permission of the publisher
except for the use of brief quotations in a book review.

Printed in the United States of America

First Printing, 2020

Gwen Cooper
344 Grove Street, #169
Jersey City, NJ 07302

www.gwencooper.com

For Laurence, always

Table of Contents

Love in a Cold Climate 13

Spray Anything 37

Toy Stories 66

Daylight Cravings 89

Just BeClaws 104

The Bells 118

Spray Anything

Homer, Vashti, and Gwen - 2007

Gwen Cooper

Love in a Cold Climate

IT WAS JANUARY OF 2001, and every job interview I had in New York started with the same question: "You want to move to New York—in *January*—from Miami Beach?"

Sometimes this would be followed by the interviewer rhapsodizing about how his or her secret dream was making the reverse move of the one I contemplated—from Manhattan to South Beach instead of vice versa. Sometimes reference would be made to the temperature, currently hovering in the twenties in New York City, thermometers struggling to rise beneath a thick blanket of slate-gray clouds that wouldn't let a single ray of sunshine through, yet also stubbornly refused to yield the gentle snowfall that might have cloaked the city in a hint of romance. Sometimes the interviewer would simply wave a hand to indicate a frost-covered window—which, to my benighted eyes, looked glittery and dazzling, the secret, overnight work of the snow fairies I'd read about in books as a child. But to the typical New Yorker, it meant only one thing: *It's freaking COLD out there!*

Spray Anything

Always, however, the question would be asked in the sort of incredulous, are-you-*crazy?!* tone only a true New Yorker can muster—as if I'd announced that, after the interview, I intended to treat myself to the finest Italian meal New York City had to offer…at the Times Square Olive Garden.

South Beach, where I currently lived, was the land of bare skin and beaches—of white sands, turquoise waters, and year-round tans. My apartment building boasted an Olympic-sized swimming pool, which could be comfortably enjoyed for all but perhaps two uncharacteristically cold weeks out of the year. A mere thirty feet from that pool was Biscayne Bay, where one could go boating or jet skiing even (and especially) in the depths of January. From the balcony of my spacious one-bedroom apartment, I could look to the left and see the Bay, and to the right I could see the ocean itself, its waters closest to shore dotted with puffy white windsurfing sails and colorful floats upon which sunbathers bobbed along and, a bit farther out, the occasional cigarette boat zooming along, leaving a barely discernible wake.

Only a truly insane person, the raised eyebrows of my interviewers strongly implied, would consider trading this paradise for the purgatory of New York City in winter.

"Hell is hot all year round, too," I'd quip, "but nobody wants to live there." By this, I didn't mean to imply that my life in South Beach could be described as "hellish." Far from it. But I did feel—with all the confidence of a person who'd never had to stand a truly cold climate for more than five consecutive days in her entire life—that warm weather wasn't everything. Like a person who's always been so wealthy that she truly can't understand why people make such a fuss about *money*, of all things, I took sunshine and soft, salt-scented breezes for granted. I didn't think it was *nothing*, but it hardly made sense to arrange one's whole life around so trivial a consideration.

I wasn't a masochist, and the decision to move to New York wasn't one I'd arrived at lightly. I didn't work in tourism, hospitality, or international finance—just about the only stable industries in Miami. I worked in corporate marketing communications and, since I didn't have a background in any of the aforementioned fields, my only real job opportunities had come from the kind of fly-by-night companies that sprang up like dandelions and disappeared just as quickly from Miami's ever-shifting economic landscape. I wanted to work for a media company—print or online ("online" still being a fairly new word in the common parlance), it didn't matter to me. I wanted to work with people who created written content for a large audience, and I had a vague hope that I, myself, might someday be one of those people who created that written content.

Plus, I'd always been more partial to cityscapes than beachscapes, anyway. I loved tall buildings, small sidewalk cafes, live theater, and quirky little shops that weren't part of a national chain. In my mind's fanciful eye, I saw myself with chic coats and jackets, sweaters in my closet (a closetful of sweaters—imagine it!) that varied in thickness, so that some made more sense for the early days of fall while others were clearly best suited for the late days of winter. I imagined suede boots with high heels that would rap confidently along concrete sidewalks, adding two—or perhaps even three—inches to my height.

There's no such thing as "living" in New York—there's only surviving there, a writer friend of mine, a New York transplant to Miami, had warned me. But I pooh-poohed the notion. New York was where I wanted to be. My twenty-ninth birthday had just passed, and my thirtieth was looming on the horizon—which meant there was no better time than the present.

I ended up receiving a few job offers, one of which came with the added bonus of covering my moving expenses. The die was cast. On January 29th of 2001, just over two weeks before Valentine's Day, my three cats and I moved from our roomy South Beach one-bedroom into a small studio in Manhattan.

THE COLD WAS BEWILDERING TO all of us at first—my cats as well as me. It howled around our new corner apartment way up on the thirty-first floor. You could actually hear the cold wind whipping around outside our windows at night as if demanding to be let in, which caused the four of us to shiver closer together (or as close as the ever-aloof Scarlett would allow the other cats to get to her) beneath the thick comforter I'd packed into an extra checked suitcase on our plane ride up. Vashti, out of all of us, was perhaps genetically best suited for cold weather, with her thick snowy fur and the tufts of white that sprang from beneath the pink pads of her paws, like built-in snowshoes. But even she was stunned into a certain sluggishness for the first few days, the three of them—including Homer, usually such a little bundle of activity—spending most of their time either sleeping or wandering around the confines of our new, tiny apartment in a disoriented way, territorially staking out warm spots on the floor for the hour in the mornings when sunlight (if it wasn't cloudy) fell directly through the windows. Homer was particularly confused by the fact that we were now living in a single room, a turn of events that not only didn't jibe with anything in his previous experience, but which was, apparently, beyond even his conceptual understanding. He seemed convinced there was a door that would lead to another room, somewhere, if only he could find it, whining and pawing fretfully at the plaster whenever his nose or whiskers encountered a wall where it seemed clear to him that a door ought to be. Scarlett and

Vashti, unlike Homer, could *see* that our new apartment was, indeed, as small as it felt. They could also tell that the sound of the wind outside wasn't made by an actual creature seeking entrance. But not so with Homer. Sometimes I woke in the night to hear him hiss in alarm as a particularly strong gust of wind tore loudly around the outside of our walls. *Stay out! We don't need any more cold in here!*

It didn't help that our heater—which should have been able to ward off any feeling of cold inside, even if it couldn't stop the sound of it outside—periodically made a startlingly loud buzzing sound, and then clanked and clonked four or five times, before releasing (evidently with great reluctance) a hiss of warm air into the room. *Buzzzzzzzz! Clank! Clank! CLONK! hissssssss*, went the heater, always provoking my over-protective Homer into wild frenzies of hissing and clawing at he-knew-not-what (some unidentifiable monster who, for inexplicable reasons, had moved in with us, I always imagined him thinking). One time he landed a full-clawed blow on the heater's metal grating and his paw remained stuck there, a single claw lodged in the grate and refusing to budge, and I had to come to his aid. Knowing nothing about heaters—having literally never lived with one before—it took me about a month longer than it should have to realize that this wasn't normal heater behavior, and to call the super to come up and replace it. By then it was March, and the weather was starting to turn warmer anyway. But for that first month, I ended up switching the heater off much of the time, preferring even the cold to all the racket.

It also didn't help that we were living in our New York apartment for more than two weeks before our furniture was finally delivered from Miami. I had ditched quite a few pieces (most notably a loveseat and dining set) before my move, since I wouldn't have been able to come close to fitting everything from my old place into my new one.

Spray Anything

The resulting shipment was so small, it wasn't worth the moving company's time to bring it up north until they were able to combine it with another. (Apparently, there were at least two of us half-baked enough to move from Miami to New York in the winter.) In the meantime, I had to make do with an air mattress that kept mysteriously deflating over the course of the night, causing me to wake up with aching bones atop a pancake-flat rubber swath that was the only cushion between my joints and cold, hardwood floors. I nearly blinded myself, so closely did I scrutinize every millimeter of that air mattress, looking for even the smallest tear or hole that I could patch up. I never found one, though, and so had to continue camping out on the cold floors of the "luxury" apartment I was paying far too much to live in, all things considered.

The cats fared slightly better at night than I did, able to curl up on top of me, or on some particularly thick wedge of the quilt, and find comfort that way. We all became very close those first weeks. Vashti, in particular, was fond of draping herself across my neck at night like a boa. I'd awaken from dreams of being smothered by giant marshmallows during a prison riot (dreams fueled by a particularly loud *Clank! Clank! CLONK!* from the heater) to find that Vashti's luxurious plume of a tail had fallen across my mouth and nose while we'd slept. Once, before I was fully awake, I ended up inhaling rather a sizeable wad of Vashti's tail fur through my open mouth and then spent the rest of the subsequent workday, to my eternal embarrassment, struggling with the resultant hairball that had lodged in my throat. "Are you okay?" various coworkers asked in concerned tones, as I coughed and retched my way through meetings. "Seasonal allergies," I claimed weakly, once I'd stopped wheezing long enough to squeeze out of a few words. I'm not sure that they believed me, but anything was better than saying, *Don't mind me—I'm just coughing up a hairball!* "How do you guys *live* with this?!" I demanded of my cats when I got home that night. I'd often said that my fondest wish would be to come back in a future life as one of my own pampered cats—but if hairballs were part of the deal, I found myself thinking now, I might have to reconsider.

I spent a lot of time talking to my cats during those early days right after my move—simply because there wasn't much else to *do*. There was nothing at all in my apartment aside from the deflating air mattress, my comforter and two pillows, a couple of books, a clock radio, a telephone, a litter box and food bowls—and, of course, my cats. After nightfall—which, its being February, occurred well before I got home from work—light came from the overhead bulbs in the kitchen and bathroom, left on continuously until I went to sleep. Still, there wasn't much light in the apartment except for the spot directly under the kitchen's fluorescent, which made reading a book challenging unless I propped my back against a cabinet while sitting on the cold tile of the kitchen floor—not exactly a comfortable position to settle into for a few hours with a good novel.

The cats' eyes glowed from the shadows of our mostly dark apartment, and I often sensed that they reflected a hint of accusation. *Why did you move us to this cold, empty place? We were so happy where we were!* "Hey—it's hard for me, too!" I said aloud, more than once, which was usually about the time I realized that I needed to hear a human voice if I were to get through the rest of the long night ahead. I'd pick up the phone to call friends still back in South Beach, lounging poolside or preparing to head out to the launch party for one or the other of this year's hot new SoBe clubs, which was invariably opening in what had formerly been the site of one of last year's hot new SoBe clubs.

It was precisely what I'd frittered away too much of my twenties doing—what I'd moved to New York to get away from as I charted a new, more serious path into my impending thirties. So there was really no reason, I'd remind myself, to feel as homesick as I did during these conversations, pulling one of my cranky cats into my arms and stroking them until the build-up of static electricity in their fur—created by the cool, dry air of our new home—forced me to stop. That I even found myself missing Miami's oppressive humidity was a sign of how homesick I was. Sure, all the moisture in the air had frequently left me with a tangle of frizzy curls that looked as if it should have adorned the head of a circus clown. But at least I'd been able to pet my cats as much as I wanted without having to worry about shocking them into hostility.

    I always ended up cutting these phone calls short, and the friend I was talking to would always promise, "I'll tell everyone you send your love!" before hanging up. Then I'd turn on my static-y clock radio, to relieve the dead silence of our apartment way up on the thirty-first floor, and release my equally static-y cat. He or she would run off to pass a static-electric shock to a resentful brother or sister, who'd recoil reproachfully (*Hey! What was that for?!*) at the little spark that flew between them when their noses touched.

BOTH THE COLD AND THE sheer, overwhelming size of the city I now officially lived in were intimidating and conspired to keep me indoors for the first few days. But I couldn't spend all my non-work hours sitting alone in a dark apartment, and so I began taking long walks at night and on the weekend. I was trying to figure out Manhattan's byzantine subway system (legend has it that there's still no entirely accurate map of all its tunnels and stops) and, standing on platforms and waiting for trains to arrive, blasts of cold air would whip through the tunnels, blowing my hair back, whenever a train was about to make an appearance. The old leather bomber jacket my father had handed down to me before I'd left Miami was no match for the cold outside. I also lacked gloves or a good, thick scarf, and even the handful of sweaters I'd accrued over the years in Miami weren't as warm as I would have liked. *It'll be different next winter,* I'd tell myself. *Next year, I'll be able to afford everything I need.* For now, though, there wasn't much I could do beyond stamping my feet and breathing warm air onto my hands as I rubbed them together, before shoving them into the too-large pockets of my dad's old jacket, which still let in entirely too much cold air for comfort.

And yet, it was undeniably exciting to walk around this sprawling, hectic, over-stimulating urban landscape I now called home. The buildings and shop windows all lit up at night like Christmas trees, promising the warmth inside that was denied to those of us outside on the pavement. Crowded as they were, though, with masses of people scurrying frantically to and fro, the pavements of Midtown were still warmer than they were down in the Financial District, where I lived, which almost completely emptied out after five o'clock. Walking through Soho on a sunny Saturday afternoon—thronged with trendy weekend shoppers, even in the middle of February—it was almost possible to forget how cold it truly was.

I was delighted to find, as I rambled along with no particular destination, small bodegas and bookstores that actually had "shop cats" in residence. I'd never encountered shop cats in Miami, and finding an ordinary place of business that had a cat dwelling in its inner recesses felt like discovering some hidden world, accessible only to a select few who knew where to look. And I also found more small, quirky pet stores than I would have thought one city could hold. My shopping for pet supplies back home had primarily taken place in superstores like Petco and PetSmart, whereas here in New

Spray Anything

York there was an endless array of mom-and-pop options—each with its own distinct personality and brand of shop clerks, ranging from morose hipsters, whose sulky expressions clearly conveyed that they were bored out of their wits, to comfortable-looking middle-aged cat ladies who were more than happy to engage in earnest conversations about which food or toy might best suit a particular cat's health needs and personality. I felt like a true New Yorker—a tribe famed for being short of temper and long on opinions—the Sunday morning when I got into a heated argument with the proprietor of an all-vegan pet shop as to whether it was healthy, or even possible, to feed cats, obligate carnivores as everyone knows, an all-vegan diet. (It's not, and you shouldn't.) To this day, that store remains the one and only retail establishment from which I've ever been banned for life. As if, I haughtily informed the righteously indignant proprietor, I would even *think* of visiting *that* store again.

Most of my encounters were far more positive, however. I was constantly finding little things to bring home for the cats—exotic new flavors and varieties of cat treats, imaginatively decorated brands of canned food that I'd never encountered back in Miami. I bought little bags of catnip and three heated cat beds that could be plugged into the wall—so that the cats would have something warm and soft to sleep on, even if I didn't. My reward was the first genuine demonstration of feline contentment I'd seen since the move, as all three of my cats rolled around on their backs in custom-heated ecstasy, high on warmth and the 'nip I'd sprinkled judiciously all over the soft plush before plugging the cat beds in.

I even bought a new kitty condo, which all three of them could climb to the top of (and finally have something to perch on in our new place), although only Vashti and Scarlett could ascend its heights and then peer down from the tops of our tall windows on the thirty-first floor to take occasional, pointless swipes at birds flying by, or gaze down like all-powerful gods on the antlike humans scurrying about far below them.

I guilt-shopped more than I should have for the cats, filling my apartment full of cat stuff as a substitute for the actual furniture I still hadn't been able to make materialize, despite near-daily phone calls to the moving company. A stranger visiting my apartment—and seeing my deflated air mattress, shoved into one corner with my comforter and pillows like a rat's nest, and then taking in all the cat toys and cat beds and the new cat condo—would likely have concluded that I was some sort of crazy cat lady who'd "gone to the mattresses" while lamming it from mafia hitmen.

Perhaps the only disheartening thing about all the time I spent out of doors—aside from the cold itself, which was brutal and unrelenting—were the festive windows of jewelry stores and card shops and restaurants, all proclaiming the imminent arrival of Valentine's Day. I would be alone this year—utterly alone in a way I never had been before. It wasn't as if I'd left some great boyfriend behind in Miami (had there been a great boyfriend, I likely wouldn't have moved away in the first place). And it certainly wasn't as if I'd never before borne witness to excited women in my office whose desks, for that one day, were adorned with colorful bouquets and heart-shaped boxes of candy while my own desk remained bare of all such baubles. I'd never even really cared all that much about Valentine's Day, truth be told—not even when I'd had boyfriends to spend the holiday with.

But this would be the first year when I wouldn't have the option of hanging out with a group of friends—to watch a marathon of rom-coms (if we were feeling aspirational) or action movies (if we felt like going against the romantic mood of the day)—while we reassured each other that we were all fabulous and would eventually be

Spray Anything

appreciated by The Right Person, who simply hadn't materialized yet, and that everybody knew Valentine's Day was just a made-up Hallmark holiday, anyhow. I was still young enough to feel that arbitrary calendar dates amounted to milestones against which I was supposed to be measuring my progress in life—and this last Valentine's Day of my twenties didn't seem to offer much in the way of positive reflections on what I'd accomplished with my life thus far.

And I wouldn't even be able to watch those rom-coms or action movies on my own. I still had no TV, no DVD player. There was literally nothing in my apartment to watch or look at, aside from my cats.

AND WATCH MY CATS, I did. I watched them as they slept in their new beds, and as Homer—creeping along quietly and believing, as always, that "silent" and "invisible" were the same thing—attempted to annex Scarlett's bed the moment she got out of it, receiving an imperious slap of her front paw as his reward. I watched as all three of them began engaging in extraordinarily elaborate grooming rituals, attempting to combat the static electricity that made the job of ridding themselves of pesky bits of stray fur and dust far more onerous than it had been back in Miami. Their own shed fur clung to them, as did fur from the other cats. Strands of Vashti's white fur stuck to Homer's ebony coat—or vice versa—and Scarlett's gray tabby tufts, which occupied a sort of hued middle ground between them, were conspicuous on all three cats. And no matter how much I tried to clean (which wasn't too hard, since there wasn't any furniture), if there was a single speck of dust or strand of my own hair floating around, it seemed to find its way eventually to my cats' flanks and tails, held fast by a static-electric charge.

All the extra grooming forced my cats to roll onto their backs more than usual, to reach those hard-to-get spots, and of course all the extra rolling just made more static accumulate in their fur. I'd never thought much about how often or vigorously my cats groomed themselves—cats' grooming had, for some years now, simply been a part of the "background noise" of my everyday life, like the way you stop hearing the crashing of the tides when you live on a beach. But, with so little else to pay attention to—without the blare of the television or a constantly ringing phone to distract me—I noticed it now. I started noticing, or at least consciously thinking about, other things, too. Things I realized I'd known on some level all along, but had stopped paying attention to somewhere along the way.

I'd always felt that I knew the three of them well, of course. I was their "mom." Who could possibly know my cats better or more intimately than I did? I'd always thought of myself as a conscientious cat custodian, able to recite, at a moment's notice, complete personal and medical histories, food preferences, sleeping habits, and so on.

But, during our first two weeks in New York, I got to know them even better than I already had—and to wonder about things that I might have noticed before, but had never contemplated the meaning of. Scarlett, for example, always kicked her left hind leg twice when exiting the litter box. She was the most fastidious of all my cats, and hated tracking even a speck of litter outside of the box if she could help it. But, even if there weren't any obvious particles clinging to her fur when she exited, she still always did that little two-step kick before she considered her business concluded. Why? Was it merely a habit? Some sort of obsessive-compulsive ritual that she couldn't have rid herself of, even if she'd wanted to? Had some unwelcome tagalong from the litter box once stuck to her back paw in her younger days, irritating her for hours and leaving an indelible impression that persisted even all these years later? Or perhaps, I reflected, this was new behavior since our move to New York, some response to our new environment that made some kind of logical sense to Scarlett, even if its logic wasn't at all apparent to me.

Scarlett was also the least inherently trusting of my cats—and yet, she was the only one who ever slept sprawled out on her back, four white paws in the air with her white tummy exposed to whoever might happen by. To make herself so vulnerable when she slept—the time when she was already most vulnerable to begin with—seemed incongruous with what I knew of Scarlett's personality. It was a genuine puzzle, when I paused to give it some thought, and one that I still don't have an entirely satisfactory answer to—beyond noting that Scarlett had gained, by far, the most weight of any of them over the years, and at a certain point she was probably most comfortable simply letting it all hang loose, so to speak.

Vashti liked to sleep in a loaf-of-bread posture, on her belly with her head up and her four little paws tucked beneath her. And she never drank water directly from her water bowl—or from the bathtub faucet, which she occasionally pestered me about until I turned it on for her. Instead, she'd daintily dip a paw into the water and then, when it was thoroughly soaked, lick the droplets from her paw. It was a habit that I'd been dimly aware of, but had always thought of it as her "washing her hands." I tried now to remember if I'd ever seen her actually lapping water directly from a water source, and found that I couldn't recall a single instance of it. And wasn't that an odd thing to notice for the first time about a cat I'd been living with for nearly six years?

Every morning, and despite his blindness, Homer unerringly found, with the accuracy of a heat-seeking missile, the warm patch of sunlight that fell through our windows onto the floor at eight a.m. The pure coal black of his fur glowed a warm chocolatey brown in direct sunlight, with tabby stripes of a slightly darker brown, and how was it possible that I'd never realized before, or even thought about, how heart-stoppingly beautiful that was? Whenever he slept in the sun, he liked to fling one paw over the space where his eyes would have been—another thing I'd noticed but never really considered. It wasn't as if the brightness of the light falling across his face would have woken him up. Was it an instinctive response to the heat, the way the muscles around his sockets tightened, as if he were blinking, if a blast of air hit his face?

Homer, in some ways, fared better than the rest of us—not only because the darkness of our lamp-less apartment at night couldn't possibly matter to him, but also because I'd packed his beloved stuffed worm into his carrier with him when we'd flown from Miami to New York. He, at least, had something well-loved and familiar to keep him company in this strange new place. I'd been cognizant enough of his love for that worm to think to pack it with him when we traveled, but I hadn't given it much consideration aside from, *Homer really likes that worm.* I thought now, though, what an odd thing it was that *this* bedraggled, slightly woebegone toy—of all the things I'd so lovingly set before Scarlett in the earliest days of her kitten-hood—had been the one and only store-bought toy that had stood the test of time, cherished by all three of my cats in their turn until it had finally fallen to Homer, who'd claimed it definitively as his own special property. As much as Scarlett and Vashti had enjoyed it before him, they'd never fallen asleep with it between their front paws, as Homer habitually did, one whiskered cheek resting peacefully atop it in the sunlight.

I'd toss a crumpled up piece of paper I'd filched from my new office for Scarlett and Vashti's entertainment (we had to have *something* to do to kill the time, after all), and remember what a very hard time Scarlett had given me with her resolute indifference to me, and to anything having to do with me, during our earliest days together, when she was still the first and only cat I'd ever lived with. For the past year or so, she'd come to cuddle up next to me on a fairly regular basis, and how was it possible that I'd forgotten to remember what an extraordinary turn of events that was? And Vashti's love of fetch! One night Vashti brought me a straight piece of paper that she'd nicked from the windowsill where (in lieu of a desk or a dresser or *anything at all* with drawers or shelves) I'd taken to storing work supplies, clearly intending that I should crumple and throw it for her, so she could retrieve it for me to throw again. Vashti hadn't been especially interested in fetch since she was a kitten—but, as a kitten, fetch had been a deep and abiding passion of hers. But I hadn't thought about that at all—hadn't even remembered it—in at least four years.

 I noticed this, and a million other little things—the way Scarlett would always use her front right paw to spill three kibbles of dry food onto the floor, and then eat them from the ground, before dipping her head into the bowl to eat properly. The way Vashti would stand in a patch of sunlight, lift her head, and half-close her eyes for a moment, basking in the warmth, before ceding the sunny spot to Homer with remarkable good grace. The way Homer's tail would puff up slightly only at its base, whenever he vibrated it with the joy of encountering me upon our waking up first thing in the morning.

 I realize that this all sounds like ridiculous minutiae—the inevitable result of a bored mind with far too little to occupy it. And, without question, it was. But I can also say with complete honesty that I likely would never have become a cat writer, some seven or eight years later, if not for this period of enforced reveries, during which I got to know my cats from scratch, all over again.

KEEP IN MIND THAT THIS was only a two-week period that I'm writing about. If it seems longer in my memory now, or in the retelling, it's probably because the swiftness and entirety of the change between my old life—loaded with friends, beach days, and a cheerful, cluttered apartment—and this new, decidedly emptier, one couldn't have been a greater shock. And I have to think all the way back to my go-round with chicken pox in my early twenties (yikes) to recall a more physically uncomfortable two weeks I've ever experienced. There were days when I honestly worried that I might be developing a hunch, or encouraging some other sort of incipient spinal deformity, from sleeping on that ever-deflating mattress that offered essentially nothing in the way of cushion between my back and the floor. By the time Valentine's Day finally rolled around, I didn't need to worry about feeling sorry for myself while looking at all the bouquets and stuffed teddy bears, holding little stuffed hearts, on my female coworkers' desks. It was literally impossible for me to turn my neck in any direction, so many pinched nerves did I have. I could focus only on the computer screen and work directly in front of me on my own desk—which, I suppose, was good for my productivity, if not for my state of mind.

Every moment when the cats actually seemed happy in their new home, I counted as a triumph. Every moment when they seemed unhappy or uncomfortable, I asked myself whether I had, in fact, ruined their lives—which of course naturally made me wonder if I'd managed to ruin my own as well. Of all the things I'd thought about when contemplating this move, static electricity hadn't even been among them—and yet, the dry and hyper-charged air of our new home was probably the most disconcerting thing for all of us. I couldn't seem to avoid shocking myself on doorknobs or the stovetop. And my cats simply

Spray Anything

couldn't understand why touching things—which was, after all, an unavoidable part of everyday life—suddenly meant enduring a tiny, but still startling, twinge of pain. It happened when they touched me, or each other, or brushed up against the metal handle of a kitchen cabinet. And how could they even escape the occasional encounter with a kitchen cabinet, or the hinge of a closet or bathroom door, when there was no furniture for them to rest on or hide under? The lack of anything to perch on—of a comfortable sofa or bed, long-since made their own with scratches and scent marking—was deeply unsettling in and of itself. The heated cat beds made things somewhat easier for all of us. Still, none of us were feeling particularly jazzed about this alarming and seemingly merit-less life change I'd foisted upon us all.

And then, just like that, everything changed.

A couple of days before Valentine's Day, it finally snowed. It wasn't the first time I'd ever seen snow, but—unless you counted a couple of very light dustings while I was in college in Atlanta—it was the first time I'd seen snow in any significant quantities since I was sixteen years old, when a high-school class trip had brought me to Boston in the winter.

Eventually, the snow that had fallen to cover the streets and sidewalks of New York City would turn yellow from dog-walkers and black from muddy boots and car tires, before being shoved into mounds on street corners and hardening into ice piles that made the simple act of crossing on foot at an intersection a difficult endeavor, at best. But, for that first day or two, it was beautiful. It was glorious. It's hard to explain the sheer wonder that a transplanted Miamian feels upon seeing a city like New York blanketed in snow for the first time. The endless, perfect whiteness of it, stretching for miles and miles when viewed from the windows of a high-rise apartment building—the hush that falls over the city, the way that all its hard edges are softened and blurred. The slate-gray of the sky before the snow had turned the entire city the same dulled gray. Now though, for just a day or two, its streets and buildings glowed gently with a kind of pearlescent aura, casting a bright gleam onto the faces of the handful of pedestrians hardy enough to traverse the sidewalks while the snow was still falling, before shovels and snowplows had done their job.

Watching through my windows as the snow fell, in my corner apartment way up on the thirty-first floor, was like being inside a snow globe. Scarlett and Vashti were as enchanted with it as I was. Scarlett climbed to a windowsill and, standing up on her hind legs like a prairie dog, batted her paw gently again and again at the panes of glass, trying to catch the flakes that danced tantalizingly just beyond her reach. She stretched her neck and craned her head to see as far upward as she could, clearly filled with as much wide-eyed wonder as I was as she took in a spectacle that not only hadn't she ever seen before, but had never even known might exist. She sat there for hours with her head turned up and her front paws pressed against the glass, only occasionally looking back over her shoulder at the rest of us. *Does everybody else see this?* she seemed to be asking. *What is all this wonderful white stuff?!*

As for Vashti, my arctic fox of a cat, something deep and instinctive within her seemed to recognize the snow instantly. I had my reservations about letting Scarlett and Vashti out onto the small balcony of my apartment (that Homer would *never* go out on that balcony, of course, went without saying). But Vashti ran back and forth between me and the balcony door so anxiously, and with such plaintive squeaks of entreaty, that I couldn't resist her. I put on my old bomber jacket and a pair of rubber galoshes (the closest thing I had to snow boots that winter) and stood shivering on the balcony with her as she plunged deep into the highest drift where the wind had blown the snow

Spray Anything

against one balcony wall. She leapt and burrowed and tunneled into the snow, the whiteness of her fur disappearing into it so completely that eventually she was only discernible by the contrast her emerald-green eyes and little pink nose made against the white-on-white landscape she created. She wasn't as happy when, upon our reentry indoors, I bundled her up and rubbed her down vigorously with a towel. But then I stepped into the shower myself, turning on the hot water at full blast, and Vashti dozed contentedly atop the clothes hamper in the steamy bathroom, as drowsily contented as an old man taking a *shvitz*.

Homer couldn't see the snow, and so didn't quite understand what all the fuss was about. But the sound of the cold wind outside was stilled for once, muffled by the falling snow, and the rest of us seemed unusually contented—and the ever-empathic Homer picked up on our mood, and was contented himself. I made some instant cocoa in the microwave and poured it into one of the Styrofoam cups I'd been accumulating in my small kitchen until my dishes and glassware finally arrived, then inflated my air mattress and sat, with my cocoa beside me, propped up on my pillows against the wall. Homer climbed into my lap, then burrowed his way beneath the ancient sweatshirt I wore until his small head popped out through the neck—which I'd cut and widened back in my college days (as early-90s fashion had dictated). I gently rubbed Homer's head with one hand, and turned the pages of a book with the other and, for the two or three hours before the air mattress deflated once again, I reveled in the deep warmth of his purr against my chest and neck while the snow fell silently outside. Scarlett and Vashti, having exhausted themselves, slept soundly in their heated cat beds.

Despite having wanted, for almost as long as I could remember, to move to New York, I'd been homesick beyond the telling of it for the past two weeks. "Home," in my mind, still meant Miami. Miami was warm and familiar and easy, whereas everything about New York so far had proven to be cold and strange and just *hard.* I had been embarrassed to admit it to myself, and had never once mentioned the homesickness that churned in the pit of my stomach, night and day, to the family and friends I'd left behind—some of whom, at my going-away party, had predicted that I'd be back within a few months. *Not me,* I'd assured them. *Never.* Faced with the reality of actually living here, though, my certainty had wavered considerably. Still, I was stubborn and proud and felt that I'd rather let myself be drawn and quartered than acknowledge that maybe the naysayers had been right, and that moving to Manhattan had been a colossal mistake.

Now, though—for once—everything here was white and quiet and peaceful and warm. Scarlett, on her back in her little cat bed with all four paws in the air, snored lightly in her sleep. Vashti had positioned herself in her own bed so that she could see the snow on the balcony when she half-opened her eyes from time to time, already imagining further adventures whenever I consented to go out there with her again. But I was in no hurry. The warm weight of Homer lying against my chest beneath my shirt dispelled that ever-present knot of homesickness in the pit of my stomach. I paused in my reading to marvel at the feeling of it being gone, and dropped a kiss on the top of Homer's head.

"You're my good boy," I murmured into his black fur. "You're my good, good boy." And Homer, as warm and contented for the moment as I was, lifted his chin to nuzzle his head into my neck, purring harder.

Spray Anything

AFTER THAT, IT WAS AS if a fever had broken—a strange, cold sort of fever, to be sure.

The apartment was still chilly and mostly empty, and it didn't take long for the snow outside to turn into an irritating and unappealing slush that even Vashti lost interest in. But the feeling engendered by the moment of grace that had descended on all of us the day it snowed lingered. Whatever feelings of guilt (on my part), of resentment (on the cats' part), or homesickness (on all our parts) had evaporated the way the last traces of that snow eventually would within a few weeks.

It was only two days later—on Valentine's Day, as fate would have it—when my furniture and belongings were finally delivered. Out from the moving van and into my apartment came our bed, our couch, our coffee table, our rugs, our lamps, our plates and silverware and assorted knickknacks. The apartment felt smaller once it was filled, but also infinitely more comfortable. The smell of new paint and varnish gave way to the familiar scent of us, and the life we'd made together over the years.

The best Valentine's Day gift I could have asked for—better than a box of candy or a dozen red roses to display on the desk of my office—was the deep and comfortable sleep I enjoyed that first night when I finally had my own bed back. If I'd had anyone to invite, I might actually have thrown a party to celebrate ditching that wretched air mattress in my building's trash room.

I didn't have anybody who I could have invited to a party then, but eventually I would. Eventually the weather would turn warmer, and I'd befriend coworkers and colleagues. And in August of that year, at the rooftop birthday party for a friend of a friend, I'd end up meeting a hilarious film journalist named Laurence. I didn't even suspect, that first night, that I would end up marrying him someday. But I did know, from the very first time we spoke, that he was the funniest person I'd ever met, and that I wanted to spend as much time with him as I could decently get away with. (He had a girlfriend back then, who I also met that night—but that's a story for another time.)

Things got better, in other words. And I never did end up moving back to Miami, despite some of the pessimistic predictions that certain friends of mine—and that I, myself, in moments of despair—had made.

But before any of that happened, even before the furniture arrived, I'd gotten over the unsettling feeling of homesickness and constant strangeness in this new place. Yes, my new life in New York was new and different, frequently cold and, for a brief time, empty of the familiar things I'd collected over the years. Yet, even still, I realized, I was luckier than most people.

"Home," to me, had never meant a precise place or city or collection of rooms. It wasn't a certain smell or type of climate or a specific piece of furniture.

For me, home was wherever my cats were. And my cats would always come with me, wherever I went. We'd never been the exiles, the vagabonds cast onto the strange shores of a cold and unfamiliar place, that in darker moments I'd imagined us to be.

It had been foolish, I realized, ever to have felt homesick. The four of us had never left our home. We'd been home the whole time.

Fanny - 2016

Gwen Cooper

Spray Anything

IT'S DIFFICULT TO ROUSE CLAYTON—a cheerful, affectionate mush of a cat—into anything approaching anger, and if you were trying to pick a fight with him on purpose you'd probably find yourself stumped. You could yank away a beloved toy he was playing with, pull a half-chewed cat treat right out of his mouth, shove him unceremoniously off your own or someone else's lap, stroke his fur the wrong way for a solid half-hour (as our young nephew did on one occasion), stick him full of needles like they do at the vet's office, where Clayton is beloved—and all you'd get for your trouble would be purrs and head-bonks and a series of "MEEEEEEEE"s entreating your friendship as he happily hippity-hopped after you on his three good legs. "Clayton's a stuffed animal," I'm fond of saying, and with his ultra-soft, velvet-plush black belly, he does bear a strong resemblance to the Gund teddy bears I was so fond of as a child. Nothing, in other words, could be less threatening than Clayton.

Even the proximity of unknown cats—a universally reliable instigator of feline hostility—tends not to rile Clayton. Neighborhood and feral cats make fairly frequent pit stops in our tiny backyard, and Clayton, from his post by the French doors leading from our kitchen out to the

Spray Anything

yard, generally takes in this sight with unruffled equanimity. He isn't fazed in the slightest even when these strange cats—upon catching a glimpse of Clayton sitting on his one haunch and observing them with friendly interest—arch their backs and puff up their tails, unsure what to make of the little black oddball who apparently never got the memo that cats are supposed to be wary of other cats they don't know. A few years back, a feral mama cat gave birth in the space between the wooden fences separating our yard from our next-door neighbor's. Far from being irritated at seeing a portion of his territory commandeered in this way, Clayton appeared ready—if not delighted—to welcome this feline family with open paws. The spectacle of two fuzzy kittens gamboling among our trees and shrubs proved an especially frustrating allure. Whenever one of the kittens wandered close to the house, Clayton would stretch all the way up against the French doors on his one hind leg—front paws pressed eagerly against the glass panes—or else promptly roll onto his back to expose his tummy and look at me pleadingly with big yellow eyes that eloquently begged, *Please, pleeeeeeeease let me play with those kittens!*

Eventually, when the kittens were old enough to be weaned but still young enough to be socialized, we trapped the whole family with the assistance of our local TNR (trap-neuter-return) group, Neighborhood Cats, so the mama could be spayed and the kittens adopted out into permanent homes. It was the happiest possible ending—and certainly the most responsible one—but, still, it was a sad day for all of us when we saw the last of the kittens. Clayton especially.

Just about the only sure way of getting Clayton's dander up is when a transient feline puts our backyard to use for . . . let's say "darker" deeds. For a good month or so, the cat who lives three doors down took to dropping into our yard a few times each week to poop in the patch of grass beneath our stone bench. He always seemed to stop by when Clayton happened to be making his daily backdoor rounds, and Clayton's all-pupil eyes would pop so far out of his head with rage (the neighbor cat's own eyes half-closed in an expression of deep and peaceful contemplation as he did his business) that I worried Clayton might actually be on the verge of an aneurism.

Fanny is generally a much cooler customer than Clayton. She doesn't deign to notice such things as *who* in the neighborhood is pooping *where*, nor does it seem to bother her if an errant feline visitor pauses long enough in his travels to give a territorial urine spray to our fence and rosebushes. (Although it should be noted that Fanny herself routinely sprays up the side of her litter box, rather than crouching to relieve herself in a more ladylike fashion, which perhaps makes her more sympathetic to spraying by others.)

Clayton, on the other hand, is invariably incensed. His ears stretch and flatten out to the sides until the top of his head is perfectly horizontal, and—squeaking his indignation as loudly as he's able (having never really mastered a mature cat's full-throated meow)—he'll take a few steps forward and backward, then forward and backward again, his whole little body quivering in outrage as he turns up a look at me that says, *Do you see this?! DO YOU SEE WHAT THAT CAT IS DOING TO OUR ROSES???!!!*

It was Clayton's consternation that first drew my attention to the new guy—a big bruiser of a tuxedo cat—who showed up in our yard one August day, about a month ago, to spray our bushes and startle the birds from our trees. Generally, those of us inside the house take far more notice of the outside cats than they do of us. To the extent that any of them regard Clayton at all, it's either with the aforementioned arched-back, tail-up wary hostility, or else with the sort of disdainful indifference that you might

Spray Anything

expect a rough-and-tumble outdoor cat to reserve for a pudgy, squeaky-voiced mama's boy who spends an absurd percentage of his day being hand-fed treats while curled up on a soft pillow in his human's lap.

And, at first, this encounter seemed to follow the regular pattern. It was a sunny weekday afternoon, and Clayton mightily mew-squeaked his ire over the invading tuxie while I rinsed out the cats' food bowls preparatory to serving them lunch. The cat outside, having given our rosebushes a thorough hosing, lazily strolled about the yard. It wasn't until Fanny joined us in the kitchen, as she always does upon hearing the scraping and rinsing of bowls that means lunch is imminent, when the pattern long established by so many visits from other cats was disrupted.

I knew from experience how nearly impossible it was to hear anything through the French doors when they were securely closed. From the tuxedo cat's perspective, Clayton must have appeared more than a little ridiculous—a hopping-mad three-legged cat, doing a little back-and-forth stomping "dance" while his pink mouth opened and closed in unheard protest. Fanny had joined Clayton before the French doors, sitting on her haunches and delicately curling her long, sinuous black tail around the dainty little feet that always provided such a contrast next to Clayton's wider pads. Unlike Clayton, who was completely caught up in policing the tuxedo cat's crimes and misdemeanors against our backyard flora, Fanny's head was down, her attention absorbed by a little feathered mouse toy that she batted around idly with one front paw.

The tuxedo cat's yellow eyes had raked over Clayton once or twice in apparent boredom as he raised his nose into the air, eyelids partially lowered against the sun, to take a few exploratory sniffs of the air in this unfamiliar terrain. But when the cat caught sight of Fanny, his eyes flew open and his entire body froze. And then something happened that had never happened even once in all the through-the-windows encounters we'd had with outdoor cats over the years.

His eyes firmly fixed on Fanny, the tuxedo cat began walking forward—with a slow, deliberate step—straight over to where my cats were sitting on the other side of the French doors.

Fanny appeared oblivious to this development. Clayton, for the first time in all his puffed-up scoldings of backyard cats, seemed uncertain. His back-and-forth stomping ceased, and he took a single, decisive step backward, the fur on his back rising slightly in alarm. It was one thing, after all, to yell your head off at someone twice your size who was completely ignoring you—but quite another when that twice-your-size someone was headed right *for* you, with every apparent intention of taking you up on the confrontation you'd implied with all your yelling.

In a sense, all the time we'd spent over the years watching the cats who visited our backyard had felt almost like a play or a movie—a one-way viewing experience, in other words. We observed the feline "performers," but they took little or no notice of us. The French doors through which we observed them served as a sort of "fourth wall" that—except for occasional eye contact or momentary wariness—was never broken. Even those backyard kittens Clayton had wanted so desperately to play with, for all his cajoling and clowning attempts to get their attention, had never given any indication of being aware of his presence. So to have this new cat not only see and acknowledge us, but start walking right over *to* us, was unnerving—like being in a comedy club and heckling a comedian who not only heckles you back, but actually steps down from the stage and into the audience, heading your way to confront you physically and directly.

I had just gotten a can of cat food out of the cabinet and, holding it along with the cats' freshly cleaned bowls, I moved instinctively to stand behind Clayton and Fanny. I knew, of course, that they were entirely safe behind the closed and locked kitchen doors. I wasn't sure, however, that Clayton himself was aware of this. I couldn't tell if the shiver that ran from his shoulders through the tip of his thick tail was heightened anger or the beginnings of fear. The thought of Clayton being afraid in his own home was an upsetting one, to say the least, and my first impulse was to make a loud noise and big, sudden movements, for the sake of frightening this strange tuxedo cat away.

But I hesitated. It's probably not an exaggeration to say that I'd never once in my whole life frightened a cat on purpose, and I found myself reluctant to do so now, especially since my own cats weren't in any actual danger.

For her part, Fanny's attention remained rapt on the mouse toy at her feet, which she continued to bat around in a desultory way with her left paw, unaware of the drama unfolding around her. It wasn't until the tuxedo cat was so close to the doors that his pink nose was almost pressed against the glass that she finally looked up, directly into his face.

Everything went still. Even Clayton seemed to hold his breath—as did I—though his gaze swung wildly back and forth between his sister's face and that of the interloper. The two cats' eyes locked for a long, unblinking moment, and I—a hopelessly ignorant human observer to this bit of inscrutable feline byplay—wasn't sure what to make of their expressions. Tension formed a knot in my stomach as I waited for the outside cat to snarl or throw his body against the glass or do something else overtly aggressive.

But the tension of the moment was broken suddenly as the tuxedo cat, finally, blinked once or twice—which, in cat language, is an unmistakably sociable signal. In the manner of a puppy, he cocked his head to one side at a pleasant, curious angle. He brought one front paw up into the air and tapped gently a few times at the glass right in front of Fanny's face. *Hello. Are you friendly?*

Fanny blinked back at the cat, but all four of her own paws remained firmly on the ground. She rose from her haunches and arched her back ever so slightly—not with an air of aggression, as Clayton had earlier, but more as if she were simply stretching her muscles a bit after having been sitting down. She didn't acknowledge the tuxedo cat's rap against the glass with any return gesture. Instead, turning her head to where I remained standing—clean bowls still in one hand and a can of cat food in the other—she turned her back to the outside cat and walked over to the spot on the floor near the kitchen counter where I usually serve the cats' meals.

The tuxedo cat lingered at the door for a moment, watching Fanny's retreat into the shadowy recesses of the kitchen with large, unblinking eyes. Then, casting an indifferent look at the now-silent Clayton, he also turned his back. Crossing the yard, the tuxedo cat leapt nimbly onto a tree branch. With one last glance back into our kitchen, he disappeared over the fence and was gone.

I GOT TO KNOW THE CAT well, at least by sight, over the next few days. He was taller than either Clayton or Fanny, and broader. In contrast with Clayton's soft plumpness, his was the stockiness of muscle, the shifting weight of which, as he strode around our yard, added an inevitable swagger to his feline prowl. His tuxedo markings were so nearly perfect that it was almost as if someone had started with an all-white cat and then painted a cat-size tuxedo onto him. He had a black mask over his ears and eyes and the top of his nose, and from the bridge of his nose down his face was entirely white, which made it look as if he were dressed for a masked ball. His breastbone featured two sideways triangles of white surrounded by black, like the collar of a tuxedo shirt peeping over a tuxedo jacket, and the pattern continued down his mostly white chest, also flanked by black "lapels." (All he was missing to perfect the look was a little red boutonniere pinned to his chest.) He had a black back and tail, a white belly, and predominantly black legs, with four little white "socks."

He rolled onto his back one day while lounging on a sunny patch of the brick tile surrounding our backyard grill, and a quick glance confirmed that he was not only male, but extravagantly male—which is to say, he hadn't been neutered. This led me to believe that he was a true feral and not simply a runaway housecat—an impression corroborated by the rakish way his left ear flopped over, which I thought might be a souvenir from some long-ago tussle with another cat. The floppy ear, as contrasted with the stiff formality of his tuxedo markings, gave the cat a slightly gone-to-seed air—like a down-at-heel lounge singer at four a.m., collar undone and bow tie unknotted, pounding whiskey shots at a dive bar following a late-night set.

There have always been women who go for that kind of thing, women who know that George Clooney in the role of Danny Ocean is infinitely more attractive walking out the prison gates with an undone tux and five o'clock shadow than he would've been if he were immaculate. There are women who see a man who looks brooding, dark, dangerous, untamed—a man who looks as if he'd be just as apt to filch money out of your wallet as spend his own money on you—and think, *That's for me*. The pull that "bad boys" exert on the sheltered daughters of respectable, middle-class homes is, after all, as old as the telling of love stories.

It's possible—I don't say *definite*, mind you, I only say *possible*—that I may have known a thing or two about that myself, back in my own younger days. (Ahem.)

But Fanny, at least initially, was emphatically not her mother's daughter in this regard. After their first encounter through the glass, it was as if the tuxedo cat had turned invisible as far as Fanny was concerned. He started coming around every afternoon at one o'clock—the time when I gave the cats their lunch, and when Fanny was thus guaranteed to be present in the kitchen—and Fanny couldn't have been less interested. He'd strut around the yard impressively for a minute or two, vigorously spray our back fence a few times, and then, with a sort of studied nonchalance, drift closer to our French doors. Whenever Fanny walked near enough to be visible through the shadows cast inside by the bright sunlight outside, he'd tap one front paw gently against the glass. She'd pause midstride and send a brief, uninterested glance over her shoulder at the cat (*Oh . . . you again?*), then continue on her way.

It was a thoroughly perplexing dynamic, one that I contemplated more than I should have as three or four more days went by, and the pattern was repeated as precisely, each afternoon, as if it were a prearranged and choreographed routine. It was one thing for two cats to overcome their initial wariness and become friends. But I racked my brain trying to remember a single time I'd ever heard of two cats deciding to become friends *at first sight*. And while I wasn't entirely sure that Fanny herself had decided on anything—it actually seemed as if the only decision she'd made was to decide nothing at all—there was no mistaking the admiration in the tuxedo cat's eyes as he stared after her (or the aggressively territorial way in which he sprayed our bushes every day, to the point that no other cat now dared enter our yard). It seemed clear that, for his part, our backyard tom intended to stake some sort of claim on our home and its occupants. Or, at least, *one* of its occupants.

Spray Anything

Sadly for the backyard tuxie, however, of our two cats, the only one whose attention he had definitively captured was Clayton. Clayton was beside himself these days. I'd never thought that anything could distract his attention from the preparation of his meals, but that was before Clayton became obsessed with our constant gardener and his daily ministrations to our backyard foliage. Clayton would stomp and squeak and kick up an awful fuss—at least until the outside cat approached the doors, at which point Clayton would dart behind my legs or deeper into the kitchen, sometimes all the way to the opposite wall and the door that led out to the front of our house. "Mommy's little chicken hawk," I took to calling him.

Once or twice, when I was close enough to Clayton to make him feel that he had backup, he tried standing his ground directly in front of the backyard cat, who, by the time he got close to the French doors, was always craning his neck around, trying to catch a glimpse of Fanny. With Clayton standing before him, the outdoor cat would pull his lips back in a hiss—not so much an aggressive hiss, as if he were preparing to attack, but more like a hiss of irritation that Clayton was blocking his view inside. *Get out of the way, man . . . I'm trying to eyeball your sister.*

If Clayton didn't like the strange cat's interest in our rosebushes, he was even *less* enthusiastic about the strange cat's interest in his sister.

After a few days of getting no response from Fanny whatsoever, the backyard tuxie resorted to a cat's tried-and-true method of getting attention: He began knocking things over. Little flowerpots and ceramic knickknacks and candleholders that we'd studded throughout our postage-stamp backyard were sent mercilessly crashing to the ground from their perches on wooden shelves or the wrought-iron table where we occasionally enjoyed a meal al fresco. On the one hand, I couldn't bring myself to mourn the loss of our potted plants, as it saved me the daily trouble of having to water the wretched things. (How I missed living in Manhattan, where sidewalk trees either grew or didn't grow, with no input from me!) On the other hand, having to clean up shards of shattered clay flowerpots and spilled soil and the broken remnants of various and sundry other tchotchkes (some of which I actually *did* like) wasn't exactly an enjoyable replacement chore.

This stratagem on the tuxedo cat's part met with only limited success. Coincidentally or by design (and, for the life of me, I wasn't sure which), Fanny had started spending more time in the kitchen, napping for hours atop the kitchen island or on a sunlit patch of tile before the French doors. And she would, indeed, look up with mild alarm whenever she heard the crash of something or other going over in the backyard. But after a brief, startled look around the kitchen confirmed that there was nothing—nothing *inside*, at any rate—that was worth her attention, her eyes would close or turn away. Even Clayton, who didn't seem particularly interested in what the cat was doing when he wasn't defiling our rosebushes, wasn't impressed by these antics.

The tuxedo cat may have disdained to treat poor Clayton as if he were any kind of credible threat, but he was warier of Laurence and me, turning tail and climbing up the rose trellis and over the stone wall that separates our garden from the one belonging to the house behind ours whenever we went out into the backyard. Laurence caught sight of his retreating black tail one evening (the tuxedo cat's daily visits by now having extended into all-day hang-arounds) when we went out to grill some turkey burgers for dinner.

"Was that a cat?" Laurence asked—having only moments earlier noted our sudden lack of potted flowers and the "skunky smell" that now permeated our garden.

Spray Anything

"That's Fanny's boyfriend, Bruiser," I replied matter-of-factly. I'd taken to calling the cat Bruiser in my mind, and it seemed an appropriate name—although I should have been more careful about that. Naming anything is always the first step in claiming an ownership stake.

It was inevitable that I would begin to feel a vested interest in any cat—apparently belonging to nobody—who showed up in our yard day after day. The feeling that somehow—maybe?—this cat was meant to be *our* cat was growing as the days passed, even as I worried about this mysterious new presence in our lives. Just what *was* this cat's interest in Fanny, anyway? Having been spayed as a very young kitten, before we'd even adopted her, Fanny was in no position to give Bruiser any little Bruisers. Surely Bruiser himself was instinctively aware of this. So what *was* it about Fanny that he found so compelling?

And there was an even more worrisome thought: What if Fanny decided to return the stray cat's affections at some point? The conventional wisdom among cat experts is that no cat is ever fully domesticated. And I knew that this—the sense of living with a semi-wild and ultimately unknowable creature—is the secret fascination cats hold for many of us who love them deeply. It might seem paradoxical to love something because it can never be entirely tamed and then—because you love it so much—set out to do exactly that. And yet, what could be a greater joy than earning the love of someone who didn't *need* to love anybody but nevertheless *chose* to love you? When you got right down to it, wasn't that the real allure of the "bad boy" himself?

It had always seemed to me that no creature could be less "untamable" or "unknowable" than Clayton. It was hard to imagine anybody being *more* transparent or human-dependent. But Fanny—with her solitary habits and endless (and endlessly frustrated) craving for the hunt—perpetually seemed to hang just slightly beyond our reach. It had occurred to me that maybe the reason Bruiser had latched on to Fanny so quickly was because he understood her in some deep-down way that I would never be able to.

"Oh," Laurence replied as he began laying out turkey burgers, then turned back to me with a puzzled expression. "Fanny's *what*?"

"Well, I don't know if I'd call him her 'boyfriend,' exactly." I began arranging plates and condiments on the little wrought-iron backyard table. "It's more like he's her *admirer*, maybe? Anyway, he's definitely wooing her."

"You've lost your mind," Laurence informed me.

"It's true!" I insisted. "He comes here every single day just to look at her through the windows. It's very sweet." I paused to nibble nonchalantly on a pickle spear, then added, "I think I may start putting out food for him."

"Oh, no you don't." Laurence closed the lid of the grill and turned to face me. "We are *not* getting a third cat."

I spread my hands wide in a gesture of innocence. "Who said anything about getting a third cat?"

"Like I don't know how you think," Laurence said. "First you'll say this cat has 'chosen' us . . ."

"Which he really kind of has," I interjected.

"And then you'll say that we have to take responsibility for him," Laurence continued.

"Which we *do*," I said firmly. "At the very least, if we can trap him and get him neutered, then we have to. We can't just let him run around making more stray kittens."

Laurence turned to raise the lid of the grill and flip the turkey burgers, saying over his shoulder, "And *that* is how we end up with a third cat."

"Look," I said reasonably. "I don't even know if this is a cat who can be socialized to live with people. And Clayton *hates* him, which obviously has to factor into any long-term decisions. But if he's going to spend so much time here, then we need to make sure he's getting food . . ."

Spray Anything

"Which will only make him spend *more* time here," Laurence said.

"*And*," I continued, "we need to take him to the vet and get him fixed and make sure he gets his shots. You don't want Fanny's boyfriend to be some rabid stray, do you?"

"I don't see why Fanny needs a boyfriend at all," Laurence grumbled.

I looked for a moment at Fanny and Clayton, watching us from the kitchen in eager anticipation of bits of turkey burger—a reliable grilling-season treat—and I remembered my own youth, when the long, long days of July and August had seemed to hold an endless, if undefined, promise.

"Everybody wants a summer romance," I said.

FANNY WAS A BIG BELIEVER in presents—every single night, for at least the last five years, she had thoughtfully left one of her own favorite toys (or sometimes something less adorable, like a roach carcass) on Laurence's and my pillows before bedtime. The giving of gifts was a gesture that clearly had a deep and resonant meaning for Fanny, so I think it was Bruiser's presents that finally won her over—the presents themselves, or possibly the abject adoration, reminiscent of Lloyd Dobler in *Say Anything*, that was behind them. If Bruiser'd had a boom box and opposable thumbs, I have no doubt that he would have stood in our backyard holding that boom box over his head all day—or however long it took for Fanny to notice him.

Say Anything isn't precisely the correct point of reference, however—unless there's a blood-and-guts carnage scene in there that I missed. And I should probably put the word "gifts" in scare quotes, because Bruiser's offerings had nothing to do with romantic Peter Gabriel ballads and were decidedly more . . . well . . . yikes.

Coming downstairs into the darkened kitchen at five a.m. to feed the cats the next morning, I was confronted in the shadowy predawn by two glowing yellow eyes outside the back kitchen doors. In and of itself, this wouldn't have rattled me too much. But just below those luminescent eyes—appearing to float in a ghostly, disembodied way through the murky light—a large, bloodied, and distinctly dead rat was pressed up against the glass.

I felt my legs go liquid and cried out, loudly enough that it startled Clayton and Fanny—who'd been following closely behind me for the dispensing of their morning feast—right back up the stairs. Flipping on the kitchen lights both dulled the visibility of the rat and brought into focus the shadowy shape of Bruiser, who was clutching the rat in his mouth. Fanny was the first one of the cats who was brave enough to creep cautiously back downstairs, and she made a thorough inspection of the kitchen, nose to the ground as she surveilled every inch of the room for potential hazards while I spoke to her in a soothing voice, trying to reassure her that, despite my embarrassingly girly shriek of a moment ago, everything was perfectly safe.

It was still dark outside, which meant that Fanny had to get right up to the glass of the French doors before she could see through their mirrored reflections of the kitchen and make out anything beyond blurred shapes in the yard outside. Once she came face to face with Bruiser on the other side of the glass, he promptly dropped the rat and nosed it as close to the door—and Fanny's feet on the other side of it—as possible. Then, as he had the first time he saw her (and every day since), he brought one front paw up to the glass pane before her face and tapped at it gently.

The two of them sat there on their haunches in identical poses, staring at each other for a long moment and blinking occasionally. And then, for the first time, Fanny raised her own front paw and tapped the glass back at Bruiser. Bruiser paused in his tapping and simply held his paw to

Spray Anything

the glass, and for a moment it almost looked as if the two of them were touching their front paws together—Fanny's black with black "beans," Bruiser's white with pink "beans"—through the window that separated them.

Clayton's general feeling of outrage where Bruiser was concerned seemed tempered during this predawn reverie, when Bruiser wasn't graffiti-ing our yard with his spray. Clayton was, however, impatient for his breakfast, and his loud "*MEEEEEEEE!*"—accompanied by a coaxing nip at my ankle—tore me away from the romantic scene unfolding at the French doors. The sound of the lid being pulled from a can of cat food drew Fanny's attention as well, and with nary a backward glance she trotted over to the paw-print plastic mat where I set out the cats' food, and stood patiently next to Clayton while I dispensed their morning meal.

"It's all well and good for *you*," I observed, as she picked delicately at her breakfast with an unmistakably complacent air and Clayton wolfed his down beside her. "But I'm the one who has to figure out how to get rid of a rat corpse." And, sighing as I dug out thick rubber gloves, a plastic trash bag, and a shovel from the utility closet, I prepared to do just that. Bruiser headed for the back wall of the garden as soon as I turned the door handle, melting into the cool gray light of early morning.

I had no immediate inkling as to where, exactly, would be the appropriate place to dispose of rodent remains. (Once again I thought longingly of Manhattan apartment life, with its handy and ubiquitous trash chutes that you could just shove things into and then forget about them.) I finally settled on the dumpster behind Key Foods, three blocks away—reasoning that, among all the meat and produce they disposed of daily, one little (giant) rat wouldn't be noticed.

I set off as soon as I had Bruiser's "gift" bagged and sealed—not wanting to spend the next several hours thinking about it waiting for me in the backyard—and must have startled more than a few early-morning joggers and dog-walking neighbors: a bed-headed woman in pajama pants, an old T-shirt, and the sparkly kitten-heeled mules that had been closest to the front door, still wearing rubber gloves and carrying a trash bag and alternating between muttering under her breath and shuddering in disgust as she stalked the streets of Downtown Jersey City at five-thirty in the morning.

Seemingly encouraged by the first sign of genuine interest that Fanny had shown, Bruiser continued to deliver presents over the next several days. Mornings always saw a dead rat or a "bouquet" of mice gracing our back doorstep, and it was somewhat alarming to realize just how many rodents there apparently were in the general vicinity of our home. But Bruiser's gifts weren't restricted to the mornings, nor were they limited to rats and mice.

In the afternoons and early evenings, I would find things that had clearly come from our neighbors' trash cans, or possibly even from inside their homes (courtesy of unattended back porches or open windows): little piles of half-eaten spare ribs and Chinese takeout containers; crumpled aluminum tins that had once held pies; empty cans of tuna and cat food; holey socks and a frayed red bra (which seemed too *Showgirls*-esque to belong to any of our rather staid neighbors); pieces of costume jewelry and sparkly things that had fallen off children's toys; a plastic baggie of a greenish-brown weed that turned out to be catnip, which was a relief as it spared me the potential awkwardness of having to go door to door asking our neighbors, *So ... um ... is this your marijuana?* Accompanying the catnip was a battered DVD case containing *The Sopornos 3*, which immediately raised two questions: First, just what exactly did Bruiser have in mind??? And second, what were Laurence and I supposed to do with *The Sopornos 3* when we hadn't even seen *The*

Spray Anything

Sopornos 1 or *2*? (It's just so hard these days to start in the middle of a franchise.) Someone in our neighborhood clearly had a secret fetish for Twinkies, and someone else had a passion for menthol cigarettes and turkey jerky, judging from the number of only-half-consumed packs of both that began accumulating in our backyard. And while, as a writer, I'll admit to always having found it intriguing to get little glimpses into the hidden lives of others, petty theft isn't generally my preferred method of doing so.

I was also starting to feel a smidgen of guilt over having turned the Key Foods dumpster into a rodent graveyard.

Laurence and I wavered between amazement and dismay—amazement at Bruiser's sheer tenacity and ingenuity, and dismay at both the gifts themselves and also the clouds of flies that now routinely swarmed around our back doors at the site of his offerings. Frequently the flies made it inside the house when I opened those doors to dispose of whatever Bruiser had left, buzzing frantically through the kitchen and around our heads. This delighted Clayton and Fanny to no end (*I'm gonna EAT those flies!*), although my own personal—and perhaps uncharitable—opinion was that the price of their entertainment may have been too dear.

Still, we couldn't help but admire Bruiser's commitment. Even Laurence began to waver in his heretofore firmly held position that there would be no third cat added to our family. We were long past wondering whether or not Bruiser had, indeed, chosen us. That he had was now an accepted fact of our lives.

I'd started putting out a little paper plate of food for Bruiser in the backyard the afternoon of the morning when he'd brought the first rat. Even if the gifts were only for Fanny and not intended for the rest of us, the fact that he was bringing them at all—added to his now-constant presence in our backyard—meant in a hard-to-pin-down yet also indisputable way that he was now officially our cat. One of the implications of deciding he was ours was that rush of feeling that comes when a cat—or any other living creature—separates itself from the general throng of "cats" or "dogs" or "children" and becomes *your* cat, *your* dog, *your* child. I found myself gazing out the back doors anxiously, sometimes, if it seemed longer than it should have been since Bruiser had last shown up. I'd never had an outdoor cat before, and I worried about him getting into fights with rats or other cats or maybe even raccoons—or one of any number of worse things that might happen to him out there, alone and unprotected.

Bruiser was clearly a cat on a quest, and his holy grail was the thawing of Fanny's previously impervious heart. She may have played it cool at first, but she was now spending a larger portion of her days downstairs in the kitchen, rolling about in the sunlight that streamed through the back doors and persistently "come-hithering"—which is what Laurence and I call it when Fanny rolls halfway onto her back, all four paws in the air and, rather adorably, rubs the back of her head against whatever surface she happens to be lying on, looking at us with coquettish eyes that say, *Pet me! Love me!* (Occasionally Fanny will "come-hither" atop the third-floor balustrade, which overlooks a yawning three-story drop, and my heart climbs into my throat.)

Technically, she may have been doing this for Laurence and me. But the come-hithering always seemed to have started before I entered the room, and—although she never looked at him directly while she was doing it—Bruiser was always there with his face to the glass, watching Fanny with rapt attention. I knew beyond any doubt that Fanny was officially #TeamBruiser the afternoon when, upon spying him waiting for her outside the French doors and clutching an emptied toilet-paper roll in his mouth, she gave him the "bend-and-oof!," which is Fanny's highest mark of esteem—one that had previously been reserved almost exclusively for me, and occasionally for Laurence.

The "bend" part of the bend-and-oof! consists of Fanny stretching her front paws all the way out in front of her, pressing her chin and chest to the ground and raising her little rump high in the air, her long black tail held parallel to her body so that its tip grazes the middle of the top of her head. It looks very much like a deep bow—as if Fanny were a courtier paying homage to a sovereign in a royal court. The "oof!" part comes in when Fanny, without fully rising back into a standing position, stretches her front and hind legs even farther and flops hard onto her left side (which always provokes from Laurence and me an involuntary "*Oof!*").

And when Fanny did the bend-and-oof! for Bruiser—something she'd never done even for Clayton, it should be noted—it felt definitive. Fanny was smitten. She began peering through the back doors as anxiously as I did, if it felt that it had been too long since Bruiser's last appearance. When he'd finally reappear, either the come-hither or the bend-and-oof! was promptly deployed before the charmed eyes of a captivated Bruiser, the eagerness of his gaze mirrored in Fanny's own. Fanny even began leaving the occasional gift of her own on our side of the door, standing before the glass and waiting patiently with Rosie the Rat, her favorite toy, hanging from her mouth until Bruiser showed up with some present of his own, each of them dropping their respective booty and nudging it toward the glass at the same time, as if they really and truly were trying to exchange gifts.

"This is *fascinating*," I'd say to Laurence, if he happened to be in the kitchen with me while a gift exchange unfolded. "Don't you find this completely fascinating?" Laurence, however, rarely had much of a reply beyond a noncommittal grunt.

Laurence didn't want a third cat, and Clayton didn't either (at least, not this particular third cat). Fanny may have gazed adoringly at Bruiser—her big, strong, wild-at-heart "bad boy"—but Clayton was entirely unforgiving on the subject of Bruiser's abuse of our trees and plants. Sometimes he'd switch from his angry squeaking at Bruiser—which Bruiser persisted in ignoring—to squeak with equal anger at Fanny. *Stop encouraging him! It's just gonna make him pee on our stuff even more!*

But Fanny was undeterred, and whatever was happening between her and Bruiser seemed—to me, at any rate—too big to be denied. And so, after three days of feeding Bruiser consistently—once in the morning, and once in the afternoon—I went to dig out the trap I'd invested in back when the mama feral and her kittens had made our backyard their home.

THE TRAPPING OF A FERAL cat is fairly simple in theory—provided the cat in question has never been snagged by a trap before (a cat will rarely allow himself to be trapped twice)—although it does require a certain amount of patience.

Our trap was a long, rectangular metal cage with a front "door" that could be weighted down and fastened with a spring mechanism. The idea is to start out by placing food for the cat directly in front of the cage. As the days go by and you earn the cat's trust, you move the food just a little farther back with each feeding—until, eventually, the food is set far enough into the cage that the cat, in attempting to reach it, will trip the spring mechanism and cause the cage door to snap shut behind him. The key is to feed the cat at the same times every day, which hypothetically ensures that you trap the cat you mean to and not an opportunistic interloper who happens by and spots the food—or something else that isn't a cat at all. Most experienced TNR rescuers have stories about finding possums and raccoons in their traps, and I didn't relish the prospect of waking up one morning to a ticked-off raccoon I'd snared unwittingly.

But I'll admit that I was, by this time, thoroughly caught up in the romance of this wild cat who might allow himself to be tamed for love of Fanny. If the price of fostering true love was the possibility that I'd have to stare down an incensed varmint or two, then that was a risk I was willing to take.

Which isn't to say that I was at all sure Bruiser even could be tamed or socialized. I knew the challenges—possibly insurmountable—in trying to get an outdoor cat used to indoor life. But, at a minimum, it would be irresponsible to allow things to continue on as they were. So I calculated in my head the number of feedings it would take to get Bruiser all the way into the back of the cage, where he could be trapped, and scheduled a tentative appointment with our vet to have Bruiser neutered on the day I thought we were likely to catch him.

I also planned to create a backyard shelter for Bruiser, which I thought I'd line with soft towels and blankets. It would be good—imperative, even—for him to have a safe space of his own, where he could be protected from other critters and the worst of the weather while we gained his trust. And I had an idea that if I gradually started introducing household items and things with our scent on them—like old T-shirts—into that shelter, it might over time ease Bruiser's misgivings about us and possibly help us coax him indoors.

There are all kinds of ways to go about creating a snug, warm shelter for an outdoor cat, and after considering various possibilities I found on the Internet, I ultimately decided to get a large Styrofoam cooler, securely tape down the lid, and cut an entry hole into one side. It would be warm and waterproof, and while I wasn't sure how it would fare once heavier snows set in come winter, I was optimistic that, by then, Bruiser would have joined us indoors.

Bruiser didn't seem to be showing any wariness where the trap was concerned, which came as a relief. Each time I moved his food a scooch farther back in, he'd gamely enter the trap to get to it. The afternoon before the morning when I thought we'd finally be able to set the food all the way in the back and trap Bruiser once and for all, I went to our local hardware store to pick up a cooler, planning to spend the afternoon building Bruiser's new—albeit hopefully temporary—home.

I was just rounding the corner of my block on my return trip from the hardware store, cooler in hand, when I saw the flyer stapled to a telephone pole. It featured a black-and-white photo of a cat that was unmistakably Bruiser—floppy ear and all. Beneath the photo was an inscription that implored: SKIPPY IS MISSING. PLEASE HELP ME FIND HIM!

Bruiser, our mysterious backyard bad boy—the cool, hard-luck drifter who'd charmed Fanny and me despite the objections from the men in our lives—was, in fact, Skippy the housecat. And right behind this swift realization came another.

Fanny was going to be heartbroken.

According to the sign, Bruiser—aka "Skippy"—hailed from the Paulus Hook neighborhood, which was a good thirty-minute walk from our own part of Jersey City. Skippy (I realized I'd have to stop calling him "Bruiser") had covered quite a bit of ground for a cat—and for reasons I'd undoubtedly never know—to find our rose bushes and our Fanny. When I walked into the house, Fanny was waiting doggedly at her post before the French doors for the mystery cat's reappearance, Rosie the Rat held

Spray Anything

patiently in her mouth in anticipation of the afternoon's exchange of presents.

Poor thing! I thought as I reached for the phone—and wondered if feline girls, like human girls, were partial to ice cream and the Nora Ephron oeuvre when their romances came to abrupt ends. I thought that I might need some consolation myself. The prospect of adding another cat to our family had been growing on me, and I was surprised at the sharpness of the jab I'd felt in my chest when I'd realized that Bruiser wasn't going to be ours, that he'd never really been ours in the first place.

I dialed the number I'd seen on the poster, and the woman who answered sounded significantly older than I was. "Skippy's been spending a lot of time in our backyard," I told her, the name feeling odd and uncomfortable in my mouth. "If you come by tomorrow, I should be able to return him to you."

THE WINDOW OF MY LITTLE writing nook on the second floor of our house overlooks the backyard, so when the trap finally sprang the next morning—with Skippy safely inside—I heard it as soon as it happened. Although, even if I hadn't heard the trap's front entrance snap close, the loud, piteous wail the tuxedo cat sent up would have been a more than adequate tip-off. I raced downstairs to the kitchen and over to the French doors, where Fanny was pacing anxiously back and forth, her eyes fixed on Skippy in his cage. *Help him!* the look in her eyes beseeched as she turned them toward me. *He's in trouble!*

Opening the doors and shooing Fanny away from them (I didn't want her to get any ideas about darting into the backyard), I lugged the trap containing Skippy—who must have weighed a good fifteen pounds at least—into the kitchen. One of the more effective ways of calming a trapped cat is to throw a clean towel or blanket over the trap, and I had just such a towel at the ready, waiting on the kitchen counter.

But I didn't sling it over the cage—not right away. I couldn't help it. The romance between Fanny and Bruiser/Skippy had been building for nearly ten days up to this precise moment—the moment when the two of them would, at long last, meet face to face and nose to nose, with no glass separating them. They'd be able to touch paws for real, if they wanted to. That this meeting would take place through the metal bars of a cat trap—Fanny on one side of the bars, her backyard boyfriend on the other—added a poignancy to the moment that hadn't been there when, days ago, I'd imagined this first meeting and Fanny's joy at being united with her true love at last.

Skippy kept up his miserable wail from within the cage, striving unsuccessfully to huddle himself into a corner. I found myself remembering my own "bad boy" from years and years ago. He'd called me from jail very late one night, having been arrested for some minor infraction or other, and as twenty-one-year-old me had raced down to the police department to bail him out—through the darkness and deserted streets that had made it seem as if there were nothing in the entire world other than me, my car, and the man I was on my way to rescue—there had seemed to be a kind of wild and irresistible romance to the whole affair.

When I'd arrived, however, his bail had been more than I could afford to cover, so I'd been forced to call his mother, an unexpectedly distinguished lady who showed up in a Chanel suit as crisp and immaculate at two in the morning as it would have been at two in the afternoon. When she'd finally posted bail and the cop on duty had brought my boyfriend out, there was a look on her face that would have withered flowers in springtime. Upon seeing his mother, my bad boy instantly burst into tears. And . . . somehow he suddenly didn't seem nearly so "edgy" or

Spray Anything

"cool" anymore. As I collected my purse and the raincoat I'd thrown on over my sleep-wear and crept out of the police station, unnoticed by either of them, I remember telling myself, *Well . . . I guess that's that.*

Perhaps some similar feeling was operating in Fanny now—or maybe, even for cats, it's sometimes true that the anticipation of a moment turns out to better than the moment itself, when it finally arrives. Skippy's cries of misery continued to echo throughout the kitchen as Fanny tentatively approached the cage and inhaled a few cautious sniffs of it and the cat it contained. And then, curling her lips and raising a front paw into the air, she hissed loudly and smacked furiously at the cage as Skippy, pausing for breath at last, flinched ever farther back into his little corner and regarded her with yellow eyes filled with sadness and reproach.

"Fanny!" I cried. I'd never seen Fanny hiss or swipe at anybody. "That's your friend! Don't you recognize him?"

But it would seem that Fanny did not—or maybe she did, but seeing her wild, rebellious tom reduced to a caged and crying creature didn't suit her ideas of what a proper boyfriend should be. In any case, she hissed again and slapped the cage once more for good measure, then wheeled around and tore up the kitchen stairs, colliding with Clayton, who'd been on his way down to see what all the ruckus was about.

"*Women*," I said to Skippy in the now-silent kitchen. "Am I right?" And then, pausing a beat to await a rueful chuckle of agreement that obviously never came, I sighed and tossed the clean towel over the cage, which seemed to settle Skippy down considerably.

Skippy's human came by to collect him two hours later, a gray-haired woman who'd been in Jersey City for decades before the mass migration from Manhattan—and its outrageously high rents—that had swept in relative newcomers like Laurence and me. She easily transferred

Skippy's bulk from the cage into the cat carrier she'd brought with her. At the sight of his mom, the cat had once again taken up his doleful cries, although the familiarity of his own carrier appeared to soothe him, and from its dark recesses I could see his golden eyes, calmer now, blinking out at me.

"You know," I said tentatively to the woman—not liking to insert an opinion I hadn't been asked for, but having feelings on the subject strong enough that I couldn't resist saying *something*—"he might stick closer to home" (*and not spray so much,* I thought but didn't say) "if maybe you had him neutered?" I heard my voice go up at the end of the sentence, as if my sentence were a question—as if it might sound less judgmental that way.

Which, of course, it didn't.

The woman smiled at me sadly. "My husband didn't believe in neutering animals," she said. "He passed away about a year ago."

"I'm so sorry," I said, and let the matter drop.

"He was crazy about Skippy," she added. "Thank you so much for bringing him back to me." And then, refusing the twenty she tried to press into my hand, I let her out and closed the door behind her. There was a wrenching feeling in my belly as I realized that I would never see the tuxedo cat's little face, with its floppy little ear, waiting for Fanny and me at our door ever again.

Well, I thought—as I had twenty-five years earlier, following another mother-son jailbreak—*I guess that's that.*

FANNY KEPT UP A VIGIL at the French doors for the next few days, peering out—with an eager enthusiasm that began to dull as one day passed into the next—for signs of a familiar tuxedo tom who was no longer there, bearing gifts that no longer came. I wondered if Fanny realized that Skippy, the caged cat she'd hissed and swiped at, had in fact been the Bruiser she'd admired so. I wondered if maybe she now regretted how she'd acted, if she might be hoping for a second chance to do things differently. I thought that perhaps Fanny was learning something that humans also end up learning the hard way: that second chances are made all the sweeter by how very rare they tend to be.

At the end of a week, a new cat turned up in our yard. He had long, magnificent smoky-gray fur and bottle-green eyes. When he squatted to pee next to our tree, this time it was Fanny and not Clayton who reacted with anger, who reared up on her hind legs to hiss and snarl and strike angrily at the glass with one velvety black paw. *Go away! That's where* Bruiser *likes to pee!*

"Oh, Fanny," I said, kneeling down to scritch affectionately behind her ears. "It'll get easier. 'Tis better to have loved and lost . . ."

Without even looking at me, Fanny struck at the glass once more, then turned to stalk upstairs in a huff.

"Yeah," I said to her retreating backside. "I never really bought that one either."

Scarlett - 2010

Toy Stories

Cat and Mouse

FOR A LONG TIME, I believed that cats didn't really like traditional cat toys. I thought that the only reason such toys existed at all was so that cat parents could make themselves happy by purchasing something they thought might make their cats happy—a cat's unbounded enthusiasm (*Hey! You actually did something right!*) being the Holy Grail of adoring cat slaves everywhere. And when the cats, inevitably, reacted with predictable indifference to the toy itself, and proceeded to amuse themselves with the bag the toy came in, their indulgent human's shoulders might sag a bit with disappointment, but ultimately they'd be cheered by the certain knowledge that they certainly weren't any *more* inept than scores of other bumbling owners of hard-to-please cats the world over.

I believed this because the one thing all three of my "first generation" cats—widely varying from each other in all other matters of personality, temperament, and taste—could agree on was that cat toys, as a general rule, were stupid. There would be the occasional hit—Homer's beloved toy worm being the most conspicuous example—but the hits were far outnumbered by the misses. Scores of toy mice and plastic balls and flying feathered things attached to strings and sticks, and all manner of other doodads and geegaws, found their way over the years from shopping bag to floor to trash can in pristine, unused condition, while the receipts for the toys' purchase (*Hooray! A crumpled ball of paper!*) were usually good for at least an afternoon's worth of entertainment.

It was a full seventeen years into my life as a "cat mom" before I realized how very wrong I was to apply the preferences of my first three cats to all cats generally—because one of the first things I learned about Clayton and Fanny as kittens was that they simply adored cat toys. *Loved* them. Couldn't get enough. They went nuts for cat toys with all the passionate ardor of a human child opening presents on Christmas morning. Clayton was partial to crinkle balls and little plastic springs that bounced zanily when thrown around the room, whereas Fanny preferred toys that resembled actual living creatures—such as toy mice, or anything with feathers.

But, ultimately, just about anything was enough to make them happy, so long as it was a toy that had been meant for cats. I'd come home from the pet store with a bag of goodies that I'd intended to trickle out over the course of days or weeks, but Clayton and Fanny would follow me around so persistently—as if I were an inexplicably tightfisted Santa Claus—and wail so piteously until the shopping bag had been entirely emptied of its contents, that it was impossible to refuse them. Dozens of toys would thus end up scattered around the living room in one glorious burst of largesse—so that our home resembled a feline version of *Babes in Toyland*—to be played with for, perhaps, a full minute or two, before my tiny tormentors would grow bored with their bounty and look at me expectantly as if to say, *Aren't there any more?* Eventually, Laurence would enter the living room—his bare foot connecting painfully with the business end of a plastic spring or some such thing—and he'd calmly observe, "*WHY DO YOU KEEP BUYING THEM SO MANY $@#*$# TOYS?!!?*" at which point I'd throw a token handful into a bag to be stored in a closet,

Spray Anything

until the whole cycle repeated itself again a week or two later.

(Lest you judge me, gentle reader, let me ask you this: If you had two cats who it was actually *easy* to make happy—who would leap and cavort with unbounded joy for a mere ten or fifteen dollars' worth of felt and plastic—would you be able to hold out longer than a couple of weeks before indulging both them and yourself again?)

Sometimes I'd get the bright idea of trying to sneak the toys in unnoticed, so that I could distribute them on my own schedule and thus prolong the cats' pleasure, as well as my own. Fanny had a deep instinct for sensing shenanigans, however, and would insist on always greeting me at the door—poking her nose deeply into every box or bag I came home with—which made concealment, as a practical matter, impossible.

The kittens had just turned a year old—thus officially graduating from "kittens" to "cats"—when I published a novel written from a rescue cat's point of view, and elected to go on a national reading tour of no-kill shelters rather than the standard author tour of bookstores. I found corporate sponsors who agreed to donate food and litter to all of the shelters I visited, and many of my readers got in on the action, too—mailing me hand-crocheted "catghans," little sachets of catnip, and the like, to distribute among the cats at the shelters along my route.

And one generous reader sent an enormous box full of cat toys. I wasn't sure what was in the box at first—it was so large and so heavy that I assumed it was a shipment of books from my publisher—which was why I made the fatal error of opening it while Clayton and Fanny were present, revealing a veritable Aladdin's cave to the dazzled eyes of my two concupiscent kitties. Nestled among the bonanza of feline playthings was a plastic bag containing, easily, a hundred or so of the little felt-covered toy mice that were Fanny's absolute favorite plaything in the whole world.

Fanny, being a cat, certainly couldn't count. But she could plainly see at a glance that this box held more little toy mice than she'd ever seen at one time, or even imagined that she ever would see at one time, in her entire life. She began cavorting wildly—rearing up on her hind legs and dancing around in circles—the sum total of all her dreams and desires distilled down to a single, fervent wish: *Give me all those toy mice RIGHT NOW! RIGHT NOW RIGHT NOW RIGHT NOW!*

For once, though, I held firm. "These toys aren't for you," I told Fanny. "They're for the poor kitties in shelters who don't have a mom to buy toys for them." It's not that I thought Fanny would actually understand what I was saying—or that she would find my logic persuasive even if she could. But I did hope that the unusually steady tone of my voice (because at least half the time when I said "no" to my cats, there was still the hint of an eventual "yes" to come) would convey that her getting into this particular toy box was going to be a non-starter.

And it appeared, at first, that I'd been somewhat successful at carrying the point. Fanny almost immediately stopped her dancing and capering, siting on her haunches to eye me with disappointment for a moment before following me into Laurence's home office—where I carefully placed the box of toys on the very highest shelf of the very tallest bookcase we had. I was wary of putting the box into a closet, as all of our closets had sliding doors, which Fanny knew perfectly well how to manipulate open. Surely, I thought, even Fanny—by far the most daring gymnast of a cat I'd ever lived with—wouldn't be able to scale her way to the top of a six-foot bookcase.

It wasn't the first time I'd ever been impressed by a determined cat's ingenuity, and it certainly wouldn't be the last. I'm still not sure how she managed to accomplish it—and I'll admit to having been filled with a certain wondering admiration as I tried to imagine what the process might have been, even as I surveyed the end results with dismay. But, however it was that she'd pulled it off, the fact remains that Laurence and I came home from lunch at our favorite neighborhood sandwich place one day to find the box lying on the floor, its contents entirely spilled out. The plastic bag containing all the toy mice had been ripped open—and while the majority of them still remained (even Fanny couldn't quite pull off a hundred-mouse heist all by herself), at least twenty or thirty of them were nowhere to be seen.

Nowhere to be seen *at that precise moment*, I should say, because as the days and weeks went by, they began to resurface. Fanny may have been a bit of a sneak thief (*may have been*, or *definitely was*?) who'd concealed her purloined goods so cleverly that I never did find her hiding place. But she also had something of the generous spirit of a Robin Hood in her—albeit a reverse Robin Hood of sorts, one who, instead of stealing money from the rich to give to the needy, rather stole toys from the needy and redistributed them to the middle-class. Not even to the middle class *generally*, but to one *specific* middle-class family that, truth be told, already had more toys than they knew what to do with, and was somewhat mortified to think that they were getting all these new toys at the expense of the kitten equivalent of an orphanage.

Maybe Robin Hood isn't the best comparison. The point is that while Fanny was indisputably a thief and a hoarder, she also unquestionably was—and remains— a generous little soul. What we learned about Fanny—whose personality, at only a year old, we were still discovering—in the wake of her first successful caper was that she delighted in bestowing gifts with a free hand upon those she loved.

When Laurence and I first began finding little gray toy mice in unexpected places, we thought that Fanny had simply dropped them carelessly wherever she'd happened to tire of playing with them. But it soon became clear that the places in which we found them were too deliberate—and the timing of when we'd discover them was too consistent—to be the result of accident or chance. There would be matching mice on our pillows when we went to bed at night, and a mouse thoughtfully placed on the bathmat directly in front of the shower or bathroom sink when we got up in the morning. If I set the table ahead of dinner and then turned my back for a few minutes to attend to food preparations, I'd turn around again to see that Laurence and I each had a little toy mouse awaiting us on our dinner plates. (Perhaps Fanny thought we might enjoy a pre-dinner *amuse-bouche*?) Laurence and I would sit down to work early in the day to find that matching toy mice had been placed square in the middle of our computer keyboards, and I began to take it for granted that—when my work for the day was done, and I was ready to pick up a good book for an hour or two—a mouse would be waiting for me atop whatever novel I happened to be reading at the moment. I learned to check thoroughly the pair of shoes that I wore most often—the ones that I kept near the front door for easy access—for any faux-rodent stowaways before putting them on, after being uncomfortably surprised a couple of times when sliding my feet into them unawares.

"Thank you, Fanny," I always made a point of saying whenever I found her latest offering—because inevitably Fanny would be waiting nearby to see how her "gift" was received.

"You're just reinforcing a bad habit," Laurence admonished me once.

"Technically, sharing is a *good* habit," I replied. "It's the stealing that was bad."

Clayton and Homer (who was still with us then) weren't left out of this Mouse-A-Palooza. They, too, would arrive at favored sleeping spots to be greeted by the grey felt and

Spray Anything

little pink ears of a tiny toy mouse. Homer was completely uninterested in these particular playthings; they didn't have bells that made engaging sounds, and they didn't smell like anything distinctive, and the fact that they *looked* like mice meant, of course, less than nothing to him. But Clayton—while not being nearly as partial to toy mice (at least, the kind that didn't make a rattling sound) as he was to crinkle balls and plastic springs—could usually be counted on to bat around Fanny's gift mouse for a minute or two before nosing it aside and sprawling out for a catnap.

I couldn't help but be touched at the way Fanny remembered her brothers when it came to gift-giving. Laurence said I was nuts, but I thought it showed real character and altruism on her part. "If anything ever happens to us," I'd tell him, "Fanny's the one who'll take care of the others."

"Good luck with that," was Laurence's invariable response.

Soon enough, there were so many little gray mice littering our home that, even by *my* standards, it was a bit absurd. I picked them up and squirreled them away, secreting them in hidden drawers, when Fanny wasn't looking. It seemed like a waste to throw them in the trash—but of course, now that they could only be classified as "gently used" rather than "brand new," I couldn't apply them to their original purpose, i.e. distributing them to the shelter cats I'd be visiting along my tour stops.

I'd known the instant I saw what Fanny had done that I'd have to replace them. I was less concerned about the expense (although even an inexpensive toy, when purchased in large numbers, becomes a real investment) than I was in getting them into the house and then out to the shelters without being…intercepted…by my wily little feline trickster. For the first time, I regretted being the kind of goody-goody kid who'd never grown experienced in the art of sneaking contraband into her parents' house.

What I finally ended up doing was purchasing the toy mice from my local pet store (cleaning out their entire stock, to the effusive delight of the owner), triple-wrapping them in plastic bags, concealing *that* in the largest purse I owned, and ferreting the entire stash into my own home office, swiftly bypassing Fanny upon my arrival back at our apartment—although the one bag that routinely came into the house without being inspected by Fanny was my purse. (*There's never anything in there but boring human stuff,* was likely Fanny's philosophy on the matter.) Behind my closed office door, I then immediately packaged the smuggled mice into a series of boxes I'd pre-addressed to shelters. My original plan had been to distribute in person the goodies that readers had sent me for the cats on my tours tops—but, no matter how cleverly I might hide them, clearly the toy mice weren't safe for any length of time in a house inhabited by my felonious Fanny.

The plan went off without a hitch, and a few weeks later my tour commenced. At every tour stop, the staff and volunteers who ran the shelters I visited would thank me for the toy mice I'd mailed them a month or so back. I was always quick to supply the name of the reader who they were really from, without going into details about why those toys, specifically, had preceded my visit by several weeks, when everything else my sponsors and readers donated had arrived at the same time I did.

Like the mom of any budding young criminal, I was anxious to shield Fanny's wrongdoing from public scrutiny.

So I'd keep the conversations light and innocuous. "I hope your cats enjoy the toy mice," I'd say. "My cat is absolutely *crazy* for them."

Spray Anything

A Fairy Tale

BACK IN THE LATE NINETIES and the aughts—before video streaming had taken hold, when DVD was the premiere format for home-video viewing—film studios would spend lavishly on a DVD launch. There were out-of-town press junkets—which Laurence, as the DVD/Video editor for *Variety* magazine, was flown out to attend, all expenses paid, as a matter of course—extravagant launch parties, and an endless array of creative tchotchkes and swag that diligent publicists mailed out to reviewers along with the review copy of the DVD itself. Laurence still has much of this curio lining his shelves, and—along with an assortment of film-branded keychains, notepads, money clips, snow globes, baseball caps, jackets, and t-shirts—he's also the proud owner of a stuffed Sharktopus, three rubber ears (one from *Blue Velvet,* one from *Vincent & Theo,* and one from a Vincent Van Gogh documentary), a box of Bernie Mac 'n' Cheese, a copy of *The Joy of Cooking* "autographed" by Hannibal Lechter, *Sid and Nancy* pens designed to look like hypodermic needles, a stress ball shaped like a woman's breast from some Russ Meyer movie or other, *Being John Malkovich*-branded Russian nesting dolls, a can of *Species* green slime, and on and on and on.

He also once had a Lucite picture frame that had been sent out with the *Swimfan* DVD (a sort of *Fatal Attraction* for the high-school set). It contained a hidden button that, when pressed, would trigger a recording and cause the frame to shriek: *"YOU LOVE ME, I KNOW IT!!!"* Laurence filled the frame with a collage of funny pictures of himself and gave it to me as a gag gift to place on my desk, back when I was still working in an office; co-workers stopping by my cubicle and innocently asking, "Oh, is this your boyfriend?" as they picked up the frame were usually in for a startling moment.

It was 2008, or thereabouts, when Disney decided to launch a "Fairies" franchise with a collection of straight-to-video cartoon movies, which I think they were hoping to make as big a *thing* among American little girls as the Disney "Princess" franchise. Tinkerbell was the familiar face fronting this new endeavor, and she was given a collection of ethnically diverse fairy friends with names like Iridessa and Silvermist. Disney spared no expense for the launch party, held in an event space overlooking Bryant Park that had been transformed into a fairyland with pink and green lighting, glitter galore, shimmering ice sculptures, a generous assortment of high-priced delicacies for attendees to munch on, and—perhaps most crucially to the success of any New York media event—an unlimited open bar.

So Laurence was a bit disappointed when he saw the swag Disney offered attendees to go home with at the end of the evening—a collection of colorful laminated bookmarks with pictures and whimsical descriptions of the newly minted fairies that said things like, "Rosetta, a garden-talent fairy, was one of the first arrivals in Pixie Hollow and shares a sassy streak with her friend Tinkerbell." The bookmarks featured iridescent glitter (or "fairy dust") that had been pressed between the lamination and the cardboard of the bookmark itself.

"Oh...they're giving out bookmarks," Laurence said, with the glumness of a kid who's gotten socks for Christmas, as he looked through his gift bag—while I, at the same moment and with unfeigned enthusiasm, exclaimed, "Cool! *Bookmarks!*"

I was obviously aged well beyond the target demo for the Disney "Fairies" franchise; still, a compulsive reader like me can never have too many bookmarks—especially sturdy ones.

My new bookmarks were sturdy, indeed, and seemed likely to withstand for years to come even the overuse to

Spray Anything

which I will typically put a bookmark. They also made a pleasing sort of reverberating *whoosh*-y sound—bending partially and then quickly whipping back out straight—when held in one hand and waved back and forth rapidly, which I discovered one day while doing just that with idle inattention while reading a book on the sofa. I was pulled from my reading reverie not by the sound that the bookmark made as I waved it around, but rather by a particularly insistent squeak coming from the coffee table right next to me.

Mildly surprised—it was unusual for her to disturb me while I was reading—I looked over and saw Vashti sitting close to me on the coffee table. Her eyes were enormous and all pupil, and she was staring with fixed, murderous attention at the bookmark waving in my hand, her head moving quickly from right to left in perfect time with the bookmark's movements.

I couldn't help but laugh. "Whatsamatter, Vashti?" I said. "You want *this*? You want *this*?" I waved the bookmark back and forth at a faster pace, and Vashti promptly reared up onto her hind legs while slashing her front paws at the bookmark furiously, even attempting to catch it with her teeth whenever she thought she had a clear shot at it.

It should be noted that Vashti was never a particularly blood-lusty cat. In fact, now that I think about it, that afternoon might have been the first time I'd seen Vashti's pupils dilate other than as a reaction to the amount of sun in the room. Back when we lived with Jorge in Miami, and Vashti used to catch geckos on our sunporch, she always promptly released them unharmed—seemingly more interested in the sport of snagging them than in anything more predatory. In all the years I'd lived with her, she'd never once unsheathed her claws, even in play, except occasionally to grab onto the fabric of a sofa or chair she might be in danger of tumbling off of. And while she'd enjoyed playing fetch with a crumpled-up ball of paper when she was little, she'd never shown any interest in more traditional cat toys, like felt-covered mice or little balls with feathered tails—which I'd always assumed was because she had limited-to-zero interest in killing any mice or feathered creatures in real life. She'd never "chittered" at birds who landed on our windowsills, or pounced on my fingers when I'd wiggled them enticingly under a bedsheet, or sprung out at me from under a bed in a surprise attack—not even when she was a kitten.

It seems almost impossible to imagine a cat with absolutely no instinctive prey drive whatsoever. But Vashti had always appeared to me to be exactly that—a cat who simply didn't have it in her even to wound, much less kill, anything.

So it was entirely novel, and more than a little amusing, to see Vashti—at long last, and at the ripe old age of twelve—provoked into a homicidal rage by a glittery, intensely girly, laminated Disney Fairies bookmark.

Laurence and I were tickled by Vashti's sudden, if limited, new violent streak. To see our sweet, mild-mannered girl, who'd never-ever even attempted to hurt a fly before (literally—flies would buzz around Vashti's head, and she'd observe them with placid, sweet-tempered restraint), finally unsheathe her claws and pull back snarling lips to reveal her sharp little teeth—to demonstrate that she did in fact have some of the same lethal impulses as any other cat—became a reliable form of entertainment for all of us. I promptly transferred my stash of bookmarks from the Disney gift bag in my closet to the coffee table, so they'd be at the ready whenever Vashti leapt from floor to table and looked pointedly from the bookmarks to me and then back again. *Wave it around,* her eyes eloquently demanded, *so I can kill it!* And Laurence—who Vashti had firmly wrapped around her little white paw, and who'd never been able to deny her

Spray Anything

anything that might give her pleasure—would sit through entire two-hour movies on the couch without ever once pausing as he waved a Fairies bookmark from side to side before a tantalized, and seemingly enraged, Vashti's face.

What I think we got a kick out of—even more than watching Vashti attack those bookmarks with so much fierce determination—was the way she would reliably rear up on her hind legs, as soon as the bookmarks went airborne, into what I called her "Abominable Snow Kitty" pose. Her front paws would swipe furiously in a *whap!-whap!-whap!-whap!-whap!*, as if she were one of the Three Stooges administering punishment to a fellow Stooge, while her back paws, struggling to support her full weight all by themselves, moved in a complicated sort of boxer's dance. "Oh no, it's *the Abominable Snow Kitty*!" I'd cry—and sometimes, unable to resist the temptation, I'd even sink my fingers into the exposed, thick white fluff of her belly, so rarely seen (particularly as Vashti wasn't one to sleep on her back with her belly exposed). And Vashti, usually so quick to preen and purr when given any sort of admiring attention, would merely pause briefly in her pursuit of a Fairies bookmark to give me a quick look of irritation. *Leave me alone—I'm trying to kill something!*

I'd thought that these extra-durable bookmarks would take me through years of reading—that the only reason I might eventually have to replace them with newer, flimsier alternatives would be as I inevitably lost them to the general havoc of books and papers that tend to accumulate on any and all surfaces of a home shared by two writers.

But, alas, it was not to be. Tough as the Fairy bookmarks were, they were no match for the persistent abuse to which Vashti subjected them. The lamination began to fray and peel back at the edges, revealing the original cardboard of the bookmark itself. Puncture wounds from Vashti's teeth pierced right through the lamination in some places, leaving gaping holes. Often we'd come home to find that Vashti, having grown impatient in waiting for us to return and wave around one of the bookmarks for her, had taken matters into her own paws and pilfered the coffee-table stash on her own—leaving a wreckage of bent and bruised Fairy bookmarks scattered about the living-room rug like the casualties from a particularly brutal bookmark war.

Things took a particularly grim turn the night we got home to find that one bookmark bore a perfectly round hole—clearly inflicted by a feline canine tooth—smack in the middle of the forehead of a fairy named Fawn. (*Gentle as a fawn, she was!*) The smiling, fragile, wide-eyed face of a delicate little fairy who appeared to have been shot, execution-style, at point-blank range through the head was a sobering sight, indeed.

"This is why we can't have nice things," Laurence observed dryly, to which I retorted, "The cats *are* our 'nice things.'"

By this point, the bookmarks weren't much good for marking books anymore. They were too bent and warped to lie flat, and lying flat is pretty much a bookmark's entire *raison d'etre.* Most of them were too limp and twisted even to make the reverberating *whoosh*-y sound that had attracted Vashti's notice in the first place. Nevertheless, we still kept a couple on our coffee table, because from time to time Vashti would remember how much she'd always wanted to murder those wretched fairies, and now that they were useless anyway there didn't seem to be any reason to keep her from descending on them at will.

One afternoon, Laurence's cousin came over with her young daughter, Allison. Allison was almost like a fairy-child herself, with long, Alice-in-Wonderland blond hair and enormous, liquidy brown eyes. Those eyes filled with tears as they caught sight of the remains of the Fairy bookmarks—the fairies still smiling with persistent sweetness from behind the cracked and cloudy remnants of the lamination that had once protected them. The bookmarks still shimmered with the glittery "fairy dust" that had been pressed between lamination and cardboard when they were first made, although there was a mournful quality to the glittery sparkle now, given how bedraggled the rest of the package was. "They were so pretty!" Allison blurted out, a single tear falling from her eye.

I thought that Allison was mourning the Fairy bookmarks themselves. (What little girl could be expected to maintain her composure upon catching sight of a slew of murdered fairies?) But the next time she came over, she had a gift for me—a brand-new bookmark. Obviously made for very young girls, this bookmark featured a plastic-pouch coating that contained a viscous sort of liquid, in which was suspended more glitter than I would have thought a single bookmark could hold. "She felt so bad for you when she saw what the cat did to your other bookmarks," her mom told Laurence and me. "She bought this for you from her allowance."

I was touched. "It's *beautiful*," I told Allison, stooping to plant a kiss on her cheek. "I love it. Thank you so much."

We were all going out to do something or other in the city that day—likely something related to my wedding, which was now only a couple of months away—and, without thinking about it, I carelessly left Allison's bookmark on the coffee table unattended as we all sailed happily out the door.

It was a mistake. I realized the full gravity of my error a couple of hours later, when I returned home to find the dried husk of the new bookmark lying in the middle of the living room rug, its plastic sac clawed open and entirely drained of liquid. Not too far away from it was a miserable Vashti, her snout and entire right flank drenched in iridescent glitter.

"Oh no!" I exclaimed. Frantically, I scooped Vashti up in one hand and bundled her toward the bathroom, pausing only to grab the phone in my other. I speed-dialed the vet as the tub ran, and put the phone on speaker as I attempted to navigate a now-struggling Vashti into the water.

It took a minute or so for the vet to be able to make sense of what, exactly, I was asking. My concern, naturally, was over whatever quantity of the glitter Vashti might have consumed in attempting to groom herself free of it. But the vet's feeling was that, since the bookmark was made for children, the glitter and the gel it had been suspended in were likely non-toxic.

She rattled off a few signs and symptoms I should be on the lookout for over the next few hours—vomiting, faintness, disorientation, and so on. None of them materialized, fortunately. Still, Vashti's poop did sparkle in the litter box like fool's gold for nearly a week.

Slap Happy

LIFE WAS HARD FOR MY poor Scarlett. By this, I don't mean to imply that she suffered from any form of abuse of neglect, or that she was plagued by some chronic physical ailment that inflicted pain and suffering. Scarlett was a healthy girl for all but the last year of her life and, like all of my cats, she was wrapped up in a warm cocoon of pure love from the moment she came to me as a tiny kitten. If you've read this far into my cat chronicles, you probably know already that there isn't a whole lot I wouldn't do or haven't done—often well beyond the boundaries of what might fairly be called "sane"—to ensure that my cats are as contented and comfortable as conscientious care can make them.

What made life hard for Scarlett (and this was really no fault of her own, because she couldn't help being the way

Spray Anything

she was) was that absolutely everything was so *annoying*—so utterly *irritating*, so profoundly *vexing*—that just getting through her typical day could be a feline Bataan Death March of sorts in terms of the sheer agony inflicted upon her.

People were annoying—loud and oafish and apt to invite more of their kind over to disturb the sanctity her home—and eventually Scarlett would have to live with two of them. Other cats were also annoying, and Scarlett had to endure living with two of *them*, as well. She shared a litter box with those two cats, and not having an immaculately pristine litter box to step into each and every time nature called was annoying. So were the pigeons who landed along the windowsills of the apartments we lived in. Maybe to other cats, having birds to watch through a window counted as some form of entertainment—but not for Scarlett. Whenever the cooing head and pinkish eye of a feathered interloper dared to present itself at a window Scarlett happened to be near, she would sniff disdainfully at the lively interest shown by the other two cats (bona fide idiots, the both of them, as far as Scarlett was concerned) and stalk away with pointed hauteur.

The weather—which tended toward the too-hot and the too-cold far more often than it hit the sweet spot of "just right"—was annoying. Food was annoying, unless it was the exact kind of dry food Scarlett preferred—and when she ate too much of it, to the point that it caused health problems and was thus replaced exclusively with a moist option that the other two cats didn't seem to mind at all, that was supremely annoying. Cat condos were annoying because you had to climb them—*you had to* climb *them!*—and who had the time or interest for such an absurdity? Cat toys were annoying, and also stupid, unless maybe they were filled with catnip. But even then they were only tolerable until their catnip smell wore off, at which point—in their lumpish uselessness—they were *beyond* annoying.

In many ways, Scarlett reminded me of my mean-old-lady elementary school librarian, Mrs. Amdore—who had, for unfathomable reasons, spent nearly five decades as a children's librarian despite clear and daily evidence that she detested both children and children's books. (Although it should be noted that, at seventy years of age, Mrs. Amdore still rode a Harley to and from work every day—which all of us kids agreed was pretty badass.)

I will go to my grave insisting that Scarlett's nature contained hidden troves of sweetness that you had to know her intimately—and be willing to break through an awful lot of crustiness—to see. There were moments when, unexpectedly and unbidden, Scarlett would come to lie gently against my leg—resting her head on my knee and looking up into my face with a gaze that was equal parts love and world-weariness (*you know you're the only human for me, but why must life be soooooo excruciating?*)—and those were great, great moments, indeed.

But the indisputable fact remains that almost nobody ever saw any hint of that sweetness, except for me. (Ah, my poor, misunderstood girl!)

Scarlett eschewed almost every toy set before her for her amusement, and disliked the idea of playing with anyone else almost as much as she disliked the idea of playing at all. But there was one game—discovered when Scarlett was roughly ten months old, shortly before we adopted Vashti—that was both interactive and that Scarlett enjoyed immensely. It was actually pretty simple, as far as games went: I would crumple up a ball of paper and toss it to Scarlett. Scarlett would rise up on her hind legs like a prairie dog and, with her front left paw, slap the ball of paper back over to me, volleyball style. I would then pick up the ball of paper and throw it over to her again—and we'd lather/rinse/repeat until Scarlett decided it was Game

Spray Anything

Over, abruptly turning her back and striding coolly away with a single peremptory flick of her tail.

Naturally, when we adopted two kittens a year apart from each other, they each in their turn wanted to get in on whatever games the "big cat" was playing. Scarlett, it probably goes without saying, didn't play well with others. Vashti learned this lesson quickly and thoroughly, once Scarlett had doled out a half-dozen or so whaps on the head with an admonishing paw, after Vashti tried one too many times to insert herself into Scarlett's game.

Homer, on the other hand—ferociously bright as he was—couldn't seem to grasp this very simple point. The sound of a piece of paper crumpling into a ball drew him instantly to my side, and, at the sound of the paper going airborne, he'd follow its trajectory as fast as his four tiny paws could carry him, his sensitive ears following its path through the air—and inevitably leading him to plow directly into a hapless and thoroughly disgruntled Scarlett, who (poor thing!) had been minding her own business, not bothering anybody, and was only waiting for the paper ball to connect with her raised front paw so she could slap it back in my direction.

No matter how many times Scarlett snarled and hissed at Homer, or "disciplined" him with angry smacks of her paw about his ears and snout, Homer seemed entirely unable—or unwilling—to heed the lesson that this particular game was Scarlett's, and Scarlett's only. *This is MY special thing with Mom!* I imagined Scarlett thinking. *Why do you have to ruin everything?!!?*

Homer enriched my life immeasurably from the very first day I brought him home. But the same can hardly be said of Scarlett's experience with Homer. To Scarlett, he was simply The Ruiner of All Things—of the games she loved but that he interrupted, of the meals she could no longer enjoy with quiet dignity once Homer had nosily inserted himself into her dish for a quick inspection (*Hey!*

You have the same food I do! Cool!), of the peaceful naps he inevitably interrupted, particularly as a playful kitten, with a beseeching invitation to join him in some game or other. The differences in their individual perceptions of their mutual relationship always fascinated me—because it was very clear that Homer genuinely believed Scarlett to be his very best friend. And it was equally clear that Scarlett regarded Homer as...well...*enemy* would certainly be putting it too strongly. But "best friends," from Scarlett's perspective, they most emphatically were not. That Scarlett might even want a best friend was undoubtedly as foreign a concept to her way of thinking as Chinese algebra.

    The thought of Scarlett losing the one and only game that she actually found some pleasure in was distressing for me. I tried to find moments when Homer wasn't around or was otherwise occupied, so Scarlett and I could play a quick and quiet round of Slap the Paper Ball. But that was easier said than done. Homer was such a very "present" cat—almost always to be found at my side or somewhere in my immediate vicinity—that opportunities were few. I would try exhausting Homer with active play to the point that he finally collapsed in a heap on the couch, seemingly too worn out to so much as lift his head. But, no matter how exhausted he was, if Homer heard Scarlett playing, then he wanted to play, too. Sometimes, upon hearing Scarlett and me starting up a round of her favorite game, he'd be too tired to do much beyond creeping over to sit silently next to her—completely oblivious to the scathing looks of indignation and scorn that she turned his way—waiting for the paper ball I threw over to reach them. Scarlett would slap him with her paw, of course, and Homer would be undeterred by this—also of course—although he would obligingly move a few inches to his left or right, to give Scarlett a bit more breathing room, before

Spray Anything

turning his head toward me in anticipation. *Are you going to throw the paper ball or what?*

During the two-and-a-half years when my three cats and I were living in a one-room studio apartment, the game was given up entirely. There was no way, within such close quarters, to sneak in a round with Scarlett while Homer was out of earshot—simply because he never *was* out of earshot. But when we finally moved into Laurence's spacious three-bedroom apartment—positively palatial by the standards to which we had become accustomed—occasionally there would be moments. I'd leave Homer asleep on the couch, where he'd curled up next to me while I was reading a book, and tiptoe into the last bedroom at the far end of the apartment, where Scarlett was drowsing alone. I'd bring a pre-crumpled ball of paper (the sound of my crumpling the paper was always a telltale sign that a game would soon be afoot, and would wake Homer instantly), close the bedroom door behind me, and Scarlett's drowsiness would change to alert attention as she sensed that a rare moment when she could play—without Homer the Buttinsky inserting himself into the proceedings—had arrived.

Eventually, we would lose Scarlett to old age and the passage of years. It was more than pathetic—it was crushing—to see how the loss seemed to age Homer overnight into the little old man he technically was by then, but that he hadn't seemed to realize he was until Scarlett was gone. Even the sound of my wadding up a piece of paper couldn't rouse his interest. Nothing did, until we adopted two little kittens named Clayton and Fanny. Clayton was every bit as enamored of Homer as Homer had once been of Scarlett—and if there's such a thing as kitty karma, then the way that Clayton insisted on shadowing Homer's every waking moment and action was surely a what-goes-around-comes-around repayment for the way Homer had once obsessively tracked Scarlett's every move.

Homer was a friendlier cat than Scarlett had been, and the close attention actually seemed to benefit him more than otherwise. He unquestionably found Clayton irritating at first, and to see his own disciplinary front paw rise into the air before falling onto Clayton's nose in a resounding slap—a mirror image of the way Scarlett had once attempted to enforce courtesy with him—was amusing. But, soon enough, the kittens' playfulness coaxed Homer back into much of his own, and returned some much-needed joy into all of our hearts.

The one thing Homer was never able to abide, however, was when Clayton tried to take part in a game of Slap the Paper Ball. He was more than willing to engage Clayton in a round of Chase Me, Then I'll Chase You, or a scrappy game of tug-of-war over a catnip toy, or to leap out at Clayton in the surprise ambushes that made Clayton positively squeal with delight before the two of them began to roll around the floor in a mock fight.

But Slap the Paper Ball became Homer's game, and Homer's only. Every time I threw a paper ball in Homer's direction, the three-legged Clayton would inevitably hippity-hop after it, bumping into Homer in cheerful anticipation of the new game they were about to play together. And Homer, in a lesson he'd learned well from Scarlett, would slap Clayton silly, as fiercely protective of the sanctity of this one—and only this one—game as Scarlett had ever been.

This was MY special thing with Scarlett and Mom, I imagined Homer admonishing Clayton. *Why do you have to ruin everything?!*

Spray Anything

Clayton and Fanny - 2012

Gwen Cooper

Daylight Cravings

THERE WERE A LOT OF things to love about Homer, and it's probably safe to say that I've paid tribute in writing to just about all of them. It would be difficult, after all, to expend nearly a hundred and seventy-five thousand printed words on a cat without getting to most of his good qualities along the way. Homer's dazzling intelligence, his heroism and bravery, his high-spirited zest for life, the harmonic melody of his purr, the endearing *clip-clip* of his paws on the floors of our homes (Homer rarely allowing me to trim his claws) as he followed me from room to room, the way the back of his neck so often smelled like warm cinnamon cookies fresh from the oven (the mystery of how such a thing could even be possible confounding me to this day)—all this and far more have been duly noted and footnoted in the two books and some half-dozen short stories I've written about Homer to date.

But the one quality that I perhaps failed to do justice to in my writing—and that I definitely didn't appreciate as much as I should have at the time—is how accommodating Homer was. It's taken nearly a decade of my being in daily contact with thousands of other cat people, and close to seven years living with my two current imps, Clayton and Fanny, to come to realize just how rare and wondrous a quality accommodation is in a cat.

Spray Anything

Cats, as everyone knows, are not generally considered easygoing, go-with-the-flow sorts of creatures. You can change your cat's schedule, his food, his feline (or human) roommate situation, his sleeping arrangements, the litter you put in his litter box—but you do so at your own peril. Your own, and possibly also a few of your cherished possessions, which end up as casualties in the war of attrition that's likely to ensue as your cat reasons, using infallible feline logic: *Maybe if I pee on/vomit on/claw up this sweater/sofa cushion/area rug, I'll wear my human down and get my way.*

But Homer somehow managed to be both the most feline of cats and also the very soul of accommodation—and if I failed to appreciate this quality in him sufficiently back then, I've come to cherish the memory of it now. Homer slept when I slept, uncomplainingly ate whatever and whenever I chose to feed him, bonded cheerfully with the other cats I made him live with, adjusted within an hour—and with seemingly little internal conflict—to any new home or environment I dragged him into, and made friends with any and all of the friends or boyfriends I wanted him to make friends with over the years. And while it's true that a handful of veterinarians would have told a very different story on the subject of Homer's alleged good nature (it takes a *lot* for an animal hospital to ban a cat for life, but in his final years Homer distinguished himself by attaining that dubious honor), expecting across-the-board perfection from anybody—much less a cat—is, arguably, to expect too much.

I always think that if cats can be said to belong to certain generations, then Homer—along with his big sisters, Scarlett and Vashti—were my Gen Xers: three "latchkey kids" with a struggling single mom who worked long hours outside the home and moved them six times in seven years, instilling in them a certain level of flexibility and self-sufficiency. It's possible that this—in combination with his blindness, which forced Homer to learn adaptability from his earliest days, just so he could do the everyday things that a "normal" cat could do—forged Homer into an exceptionally tractable, roll-with-the-changes kind of cat.

Clayton and Fanny, on the other hand, are my Millennials. Laurence and I did move with them once when they were just over a year old. But, aside from that early trauma, for the past six years they've lived in the same pleasant, roomy home with a stable couple of work-at-home caretakers who've painstakingly nurtured, probably spoiled, and unquestionably helicopter-parented them to within an inch of their lives.

Clayton and Fanny expect life to bend to their needs and whims, and it never seems to occur to them that it might, in fact, be their needs and whims that ought to bend to the necessities of life. In fairness, it's hard to argue with their conclusions when this has so routinely been how things have worked out for them. At any rate, they are most definitely *not* go-with-the-flow cats. Every hiccup in their lives is an ordeal, even the slightest change in their routines experienced as a profound crisis.

Never is this more apparent than each year in November, when the clocks go back an hour at the end of Daylight Savings Time and all hell breaks loose.

SEASONAL CHANGES ARE SUBTLE IN Miami, which is where I'm from originally. I've lived in the Northeast for nearly eighteen years now, and I still experience an almost childlike glee in the beginning of fall. When the leaves change from green to gold and jackets make their first appearances, when it's time to begin stockpiling logs for the fireplace and maybe add a shot of Bailey's to a cup of after-dinner coffee, my heart zings in my chest. And it's not just the change in the outdoor shrubbery's palette, or the sharp drops in temperature, that announces the turning of the year so much more conspicuously up here than back home. Miami's much closer to the Equator than New York, which means that—even with Daylight Savings Time in the summer and its end in the fall—the seasonal differences in sunrise and sunset aren't all that dramatic. At the very height of the summer solstice, sunset in Miami occurs perhaps two hours later than it does at the winter solstice—which is certainly noticeable, but nothing like the five-hour difference we see up north.

 The shorter days here are *much* shorter days; and, even without the change in their feeding schedule (trust me, we'll get to the change in their feeding schedule) the effects on Clayton's and Fanny's daily routines still throw them for a loop each year in mid-fall, despite the fact that these very same changes have occurred routinely every single year of their lives.

 After eating his breakfast at five a.m., and then sleeping it off for a couple of hours, Clayton likes to station himself in our living room's bay window every morning, to watch the commuters as they stream past our house on their way to catch trains into the city. As the days get shorter and sunrise occurs later, inevitably this daily exodus begins while it's still dark out—and, every year, Clayton seems to take this as a personal affront. He'll be roused from a deep sleep by the sounds of footsteps and people chattering into cell phones outside, at which point Clayton scurry-hops to the window with all the fluster and flurry of a rent-a-cop caught napping on the job. *It's not time yet! What are they doing here so early?!!?* His own internal clock is, after all, synchronized to the movements of the sun, and therefore far more reliable than imperfect human timekeepers with their abstract notions of *this* o'clock and *that* o'clock. If anybody's wrong here, clearly it's everyone else and not my cat, who accordingly takes to scolding these off-time fools for their error, stamping his three little feet back and forth and squeaking an indignant

Meeeeeeee! at them at the top of his lungs. *Hey! You're not supposed to be walking past our house this early!* Every so often, passersby will pause to stare or point at the furious three-legged black cat in the bay window, while I experience a twinge of the same mortification I might feel if my mother-in-law, wearing curlers and brandishing a rolling pin, were standing in front of our house shouting, *Get off my lawn!*

I wake up so early in part because I like to write first thing in the morning. But with all the hubbub of Clayton's re-education initiatives, I have to wait until well past sun-up before I'm able to recover the quiet I need in order to get the day's writing underway. Fortunately, it only takes a week or two for Clayton to give up as a lost cost his scrupulous efforts to teach humans how to tell time, and I'm left to the serenity of my silent mornings once again.

The high point of Fanny's everyday routine occurs at the opposite end of the day—at night, when I head upstairs to bed. Fanny loves to race up the stairs ahead of me, leap into the middle of the bed, and then pace its perimeter impatiently as I change into my pajamas. Once I'm settled in under the covers and propped up against the pillows, she climbs onto my chest for the half-hour of intense scratching and petting she requires before she'll finally allow me to nod off.

The earlier advent of sunset would undoubtedly tinker with her Circadian rhythms regardless. But the combination of that plus the clocks going back an hour means that, in the early days of November, Fanny will station herself at the bottom of the stairs starting at around seven. (I may not put in as many late nights as I did back in my twenties, but it still seems unkind of Fanny to hasten my aging process by suggesting a seven o'clock bedtime.) Every time I walk past the staircase—on my way to or from the bathroom, or going downstairs to grab something from the kitchen, rather than upstairs to hit the hay—Fanny excitedly darts about halfway up the stairs toward the bedroom before she realizes I'm not following. Upon noting that my decidedly heavier tread can't be heard behind her own dainty feline footsteps, she slowly turns and walks back down to the base of the stairs, her head slumping in disappointment, and turns upon me a look of such round-eyed sadness that it would take someone made of far sterner stuff than I am to avoid feeling like an ogre. *Oh...I guess you weren't looking forward to cuddling with me as much as I was looking forward to cuddling with you.* She then spends the next few hours, until I finally do go up, waiting patiently at the foot of the stairs, assuming an air of wounded martyrdom that really should earn her an Oscar the moment the Academy creates a new category for animal performances.

I can't quite bring myself to pack it in for the night before primetime TV has even started, just to please Fanny. But I do find that I end up dispensing treats and catnip with a much freer hand during those first two weeks in November, while the cats are still adjusting to the end of Daylight Savings Time, than I do at any other point during the year. *I'll give you anything you want—just please, PLEASE stop looking so sad!*

These are little things, perhaps not even worth noticing in and of themselves, although they're joined by innumerable other small adjustments that my cats—and I, by extension—have to make in transitioning from summer to autumn. The sun falls through the windows of my little writing nook differently in the autumn and winter than it does in spring and summer. The stack of my own books that I like to keep on my desk next to my computer—so that I can refer back to them as I write—ends up square in the middle of a sunny patch that isn't there in the warmer months. It makes an ideal sunbathing spot for a couple of cats who like to drowse near their human mom while she works, so naturally I end up moving the books to a less-convenient spot on a shelf behind me, until March, when the sun patterns change once again.

The pretty glass vase and tiny Tiffany lamp that rest behind my laptop computer are now struck directly by the sunlight that only hits them at oblique angles in the summer—which means they throw merry, rainbow colored glares of light against the walls and ceiling. It's lovely to see—or *I* think it is, anyway.

But something about rainbows seems to inspire my cats with a murderous rage. Perhaps, unbeknownst to me, they were traumatized in some way by a rainbow in their early kittenhood? Whatever the reasoning behind it, there's no mistaking their lethal intentions whenever they see one. *Ooh…it's so pretty! WE MUST KILL IT!!!* Fanny and Clayton leap like things possessed all over my desk and my lap as they try *again* and *again*—alas! always without success!—to capture and dismember the refracted sunbeams once and for all. "You guys, it's just *light*," I'll plead, Fanny's hind claws drawing blood from my thighs as she leaps ceiling-ward off of my lap with all her might. "There's nothing *there* for you to catch."

But it always ends the same way—with me hauling out the first-aid kid and then reluctantly removing vase and lamp from my desk altogether, resigning myself to a long winter of overhead lighting once the sun, a little earlier each evening, has gone down.

And yet, I would take the darkness, the scoldings, and the scratches any day of the week and twice on Sunday if only—if only!—doing so would somehow get me off the hook at mealtimes. You might be thinking, *Come on—meals that are only off-schedule by an hour can't be* that *big a deal.* And you would be very, very wrong.

AND IT'S HERE THAT I must present a self-defense of sorts—one that I've repeated ad infinitum to my cats over the years, but the rationality of which they've proven stubbornly immune to. It doesn't help that, in this case, my furry little judge and jury are also my chief prosecutors—and the star witnesses for the prosecution as well. Somehow it always seems that I've been tried, convicted of Animal Cruelty in the First Degree, and sentenced to some indefinite period of feline servitude before I've gotten the chance to mount even a rudimentary defense on my own behalf.

But surely you, gentle reader—you who have traveled down so many of the same roads with your own cats as I have with mine—will judge me more kindly. Undoubtedly you'll see that I'm not a monster, not the world's worst cat mom, that I do the very best I can for my cats and every bit as much as any one of you would do for your own, so help me God.

Let the defense show, in the first place, that I feed my cats three meals a day, serving them punctually at five a.m., one p.m., and nine p.m. It should also be noted that, once upon a time in the distant past, Fanny and Clayton were fed at six a.m., two p.m., and ten p.m. But then, in November of 2015, I was working furiously on a self-published sequel to *Homer's Odyssey* that I intended to release in time for the holiday gift-giving season. I didn't have the mental bandwidth to both meet my writing deadline and also tolerate my cats' early-morning chest stompings and mid-afternoon howls of anguish—not to mention the two of them hopping angrily around my desk chair and caterwauling in unison at what they *thought* was their two o'clock lunchtime or ten o'clock dinnertime, but was actually, now that the clocks had gone back, one o'clock and nine o'clock, respectively. So their feeding times went back an hour that November, and an hour back they have remained to this day.

The defense would further like the record to reflect that the majority of cats do *not* receive three meals a day. Most cats live with humans who have sensible real jobs in offices or schools or stores, and who therefore don't fritter away their days scribbling about their cats and posting on social media from home the way I do. How many among us have the luxury of being home often enough to personally serve their cats three delicious, nutritionally balanced meals each and every day? (The prosecution is piping in here to claim that "delicious" is a debatable point, as my cats reserve the right at any given time to find repulsive even a flavor of food they loved with wild enthusiasm only days earlier. But "nutritionally balanced" is a more objective standard, and the defense will stand by it.)

The scrumptiousness or otherwise of their food notwithstanding (*Yuck—steak and lobster* again*?!!?* my cats tell me eloquently with their squinted eyes and crinkling noses, before storming off in disgust), Clayton and Fanny pretty much live the pampered lives of cruise ship passengers. They spend their days napping and being shuffled from one extravagant meal to the next. To pass the time, they engage in various recreational activities— rolling around in catnip, frolicking with Da Bird, watching "cat TV," i.e. the birds congregating at the feeders I've attached to the outside of our windows for my cats' entertainment—arranged for them by their attentive cruise director (that would be me) before heading off to eat or nap, or eat and *then* nap, once again. Most of us would pay good money, is what I'm saying, to enjoy for a mere ten days the lifestyle my Clayton and Fanny get to enjoy every blessed day of their charmed lives.

I beseech you, ladies and gentlemen of the jury: are these lavish attentions the actions of a monster?

I know that Scarlett, Vashti, and Homer would have thought they'd been transported to some feline fairyland of flowing abundance and never-ending catnip if they'd gone to sleep one afternoon, during the first half of their lives, and awakened to find themselves the sole concern of a devoted stay-at-home cat mom, who served them an array of meals in tempting and exotic flavors at three precise intervals every day. When they were Clayton and Fanny's age, I don't think it would have occurred to them that such an extravagance—the stuff of cat daydreams—was even possible.

But Scarlett, Vashti, and Homer weren't raised to quite the same standards or expectations as Clayton and Fanny have been. They got one flavor of dry food and one flavor of moist food for pretty much their entire lives—which only changed once, when Vashti was around eight and developed food allergies, at which point we had to find her a new protein source. Scarlett and Homer ate Vashti's new hypo-allergenic food right along with her, without even a whisper of a complaint, and I doubt very much that it would even have occurred to them that complaining might be warranted.

In fairness to my current cats, though, my first-generation brood did have it easier in some ways. In the ignorant days of my youth—before I knew the health risks associated with a diet made up primarily of dry cat food—I had some down for the cats essentially all the time. "Free grazing" felines, who were able to eat whenever they felt like it regardless of what time it was, wouldn't have found the relatively minor difference of one hour's change forward or backward in their human's schedule particularly earth shaking.

"Earth shaking" seems like the right expression here, because what Clayton and Fanny do to the kitchen every year during the first two weeks of November ends up looking like the aftermath of an earthquake. I'll head downstairs at five in the morning (which my cats now believe is the unreasonably late hour of six) or at one in the afternoon to find that—in the unbearable agony of having to wait *one whole hour* longer for a meal than they think they should have to—my two little miscreants have dumped over their water bowl, knocked their flat food dishes (thoughtfully purchased by me to ensure they're never subjected to the "whisker fatigue" that a deeper bowl might inflict) under the refrigerator, pulled my row of cookbooks down from their shelf above the counter, thrown tchotchkes and tissue boxes and my recipe folder off of the kitchen island, tossed the newspapers we've put aside for recycling all over the floor, spilled out the containers we keep our coffee and pasta in, clawed the roll of paper towels to shreds, and engaged in various other acts of feline vandalism, both large and small.

What? their defiant gazes demand when I finally do make it to the kitchen. *If you weren't so cruel to us, we wouldn't have to resort to this.*

So there I am, before the sun has even come up, faced with at least a half-hour's worth of sponging and mopping and tidying up—and with no greater reward for my efforts than having my two adorable, fuzzy little troublemakers creep into my lap, once their bellies are finally full and satisfied, for a round of cuddles and scritches before they drift off into the day's first purring, contented nap.

It seems like a lot of drama over a mere one-hour discrepancy.

And that's just what happens in the kitchen! If it's lunchtime and I'm working at my desk—teeth gritted as I silently repeat my mantra of, *I will not give in. I will NOT give in!*—they'll send any printed-out manuscripts on the desk next to me skittering merrily into the air, walk across my computer keyboard, nip at my hips and legs, all the while sending up a chorus of alternatively pissed-off and plaintive cries. Or if it's evening and I'm watching TV or reading a book, they'll stand in front of the TV screen, attempt to swat the book from my hands, all while raising such a ruckus of cries and cajolings that it's amazing the neighbors have never complained. Fanny's meows take on a decidedly confrontational edge (*J'accuse!*), while Clayton opts for pathos. *Doncha love us anymore, mom?* his sad, sad string of mews—eventually fading in volume as the weakness of starvation (because of an hour! *one* hour!)—begins to set in. *Why don't you love us anymore?*

I love my cats—I do! I love them like crazy!—and I would do anything in the world for them. Surely—*surely*—you, my readers, can see that.

But I won't knuckle under on this one. I won't do it. I won't give them lunch at noon, or start getting up at four a.m. to feed them breakfast. Because where would it end? This year's four a.m. would become next year's three a.m. once the clocks go back again, and then the following year's two a.m. Eventually I'd be getting up to feed them breakfast *literally* before I'd gone to bed the night before!

The madness has to stop somewhere! *Somebody* has to hold the line, to keep our lives from descending into the chaos that would reign if my two little would-be dictators had their druthers!

And if these are the actions of an ogre, ladies and gentlemen of the jury, then what can I say? Condemn me if you must and hang me high.

But know as you do so that I'm taking this stand not only on my own behalf, but for all of you as well. Undoubtedly some of you have fought this same fight and thought that you were fighting it alone. Know, then, that you have an ally in me—someone who will stand by your side and go to the mat for you as we battle against this one, just this *one*, encroachment on our lives and liberties by the fuzzy feline overlords to whom we've given so much of ourselves already. Is one measly hour of sleep in the morning really so much to ask? If the answer is no, and I believe that it is, then we must stand together—firm and united—if we're ever to enter the golden Promised Land of adequate sleep. And I will mount that hangman's scaffold, brothers and sisters, with my head held high, knowing the glory of the cause for which I fight.

It is a far, far better thing that I do, than I have ever done; it is a far, far better rest that I go to (one blissfully uninterrupted by the yowling of hungry cats) than I have ever known.

And, with that, the defense rests.

IT'S POSSIBLE THAT I'VE ALLOWED myself to get a *weeeeee* bit carried away (ahem). Truth be told, I've never been a huge fan of Daylight Savings Time—or, at least, the ending of Daylight Savings Time, when the clocks go back an hour. It's nice in theory to get an extra hour on a Sunday, but that extra hour comes in the middle of the night. What usually happens is that my body wakes me up at what it thinks is five a.m., but is now actually four, and I lie there for an hour trying my best to ignore my cats' desperate pleas for breakfast and willing myself to fall back asleep, so as to adjust to the new schedule as quickly as possible. I then spend the rest of the day, and the next few days, in a bit of a daze because, y'know, I've been up since *four o'clock a.m.*—which is a tad on the early side, even for me.

Apparently, I'm not alone in wishing that the clocks never had to go backward. The American Academy of Sleep Medicine reports that "falling back" can cause drowsiness for weeks after the change, and there's even been some research that's tied it to an increase in traffic accidents and heart attacks. The costs, both human and feline, of this arbitrary change to everybody's schedule are mounting up.

Recently I read that voters in California, in the last election, had overwhelmingly supported Proposition 7, which would make Daylight Savings Time permanent.

Spray Anything

There would be one last spring forward, after which the great state of California would never fall back again. If the ballot measure ends up getting the approval of the state congress and clearing various bureaucratic hurdles, the people of California will have one extra hour of sunshine—with which to enjoy some additional sunbathing, tend their gardens, and engage in other outdoor activities—all year round.

More importantly, the cat moms and dads of California will never again be awakened at ungodly early hours by the plaintive cries of put-upon cats who, when you get right down to it, only want what everybody wants—meals that are served reliably on schedule. Never again will they have their kitchens and desks trashed by fussy felines expressing distress in the only way cats know how. Peace and serenity will reign between cats and humans—or, at least, it will until the next time somebody decides to change the brand of their cats' litter, or to move a beloved kitty condo from one window to another, at which point the battle will begin anew.

There's an obvious wisdom in all this, to which I can only add one thing:

California, here I come.

Homer - 2008

Just BeClaws

THERE'S A CAT IN OUR neighborhood who I've become somewhat obsessed with. His name is Oliver, and he's a gorgeous, fluffy tuxedo cat with huge green eyes (that are, rather adorably, a teensy bit crossed) and a glorious black bottle-brush tail. He's an indoor/outdoor cat who appears to belong to the people who live right across the street from us, although the scuttlebutt on the block is that, while only one house takes him in at night, there are two families that feed him.

Oliver is perhaps best described as a cat of ambivalent desires. I see him through the front windows of my home as he forlornly runs after anyone who talks to him, or even so much as looks at him, begging for attention. The softest beckoning *pss-pss-pss* sound from me will bring him flying across the street and all the way up the steep flight of stairs leading to my front door, where Oliver will immediately begin cavorting about my ankles and shins in a cat's age-old *pleeeeeeeeease pet me!* dance. If I lower my hand, he'll rise halfway up on his hind legs to thrust the top of his head eagerly into it, purring to beat the band.

The first couple of weeks we were here, it would break my heart to see Oliver chasing hopefully after first one passerby, then another, and be ignored nearly every single time. What kind of neighborhood had I moved into, I wondered? What kind of people would so callously brush off a love-starved cat who was all but abjectly pleading for the merest scrap of affection? Unable to bear it, I finally headed out one afternoon armed with a bag of salmon-flavored Greenies and a determination to bestow upon this neglected kitty some of the cuddles he so clearly craved.

I found Oliver in our back yard, as it happened, where he'd managed to corner a squirrel, despite the forewarning provided by the pink belled collar he wears. The rattle of the treats bag drew his attention away from the beleaguered squirrel and he raced over to me, but he ignored the treats I sprinkled liberally onto our back deck. I was touched to see that it apparently wasn't the treats at all that had interested him, but rather *me*, myself, that had brought him across the yard.

As Oliver rubbed furiously around my ankles, I crouched down to pet him, which he seemed to enjoy enthusiastically for about thirty seconds or so. And then, without warning, he let out an enraged hiss and slashed furiously at my bare legs with his claws. Figuring I'd inadvertently startled him or hit a sensitive spot—and not wanting to alarm him any further—I remained hunkered down on my ankles, slowly withdrew my hand, and waited quietly until Oliver approached me again. He did so while also doing everything in a cat's power—via rubbing, purring, and insistent head bonks—to indicate, *I want petting NOW!*

It pains me (literally) to report that this second attempt ended almost exactly the way the first one had, except that this time Oliver's claws landed in a slightly different spot. By the time I finally abandoned the effort and, sadder but wiser, headed back inside, my legs looked like two blood-streaked scratching posts. It occurred to me that I might have been unfair in my original assessment of my neighbors' callousness—and, in fact, I would later confirm that Oliver was notorious for blocks around for precisely this MO.

Spray Anything

It's a pattern that's repeated itself numerous times in the months since then. Sometimes it's my hands and arms that take the worst abuse, sometimes my shins and knees—but, inevitably, the essential result is always the same. The scratchings are unpleasant, but I am, perhaps, stupid in my desire to help this cat overcome whatever emotional block it is that makes him chase away the very affection he's clearly so desperate for. For a cat to crave love so profoundly, yet never attain it, strikes me as an unbearable tragedy—and what are we on this earth for if not, at least in part, to rewrite real life's tragedies with happy endings?

Laurence doesn't take quite so philosophical a view of the situation, and the last time I came in with ribbons of blood running down my legs, heading for the medicine chest and a tube of Neosporin, he was downright furious.

"Leave that cat alone!" he shouted. "He obviously wants to be left alone."

"But he *doesn't*," I insisted. "You see how he begs for attention. He won't spook so easily once he knows there's someone he's safe with."

"You have no idea what you're doing," Laurence informed me. "You're not a professional."

"I mean...I'm *kind* of a professional," I said. "It says so right on our tax return." Which is true. Every year, when we file our paperwork with the IRS, in the blank space where it asks for my occupation, our accountant always writes in *Cat Author/Expert*.

"You know what I mean," Laurence grumbled, and I immediately retorted, "No, I *don't* know what you mean," and by that point we'd so clearly devolved into one of those *Are not!/Am so!* arguments that never reach any kind of satisfying resolution, it seemed best to discontinue the conversation altogether.

Laurence and I will never see eye to eye on this one. He sees Oliver as a lost cause. I, however, refuse to give up hope.

And I've got the scabby, clawed-up shins to prove it.

JUST REMEMBER, MY MOTHER USED to tell my sister and me, *skin grows back. Clothing and furniture don't.*

This was always said in reference to our dogs, some of whom over the years combined a propensity for jumping up on you enthusiastically with a reluctance to allow their claws to be trimmed—which was especially problematic, say, late in the life of a larger dog, when poor balance, combined with those other two factors, ultimately created a situation wherein *something* was going to end up with claw marks. It was only a question of what, specifically, that something would be. My mother's point was that we should try to angle our jumping dogs' claw-y fervor so that our arms and legs—rather than our clothes or nearby furniture—took the brunt of it.

Parents had different philosophies about such things back then than the "helicopter" parents of today.

All of our dogs were rescues, and most of them came to us from abusive situations—which meant that we had more than our fair share of dogs who, in working through their understandable anxiety, would sometimes claw up furniture or rugs. My mother, who did love our dogs dearly, would nevertheless occasionally lament that she couldn't fix up our house the way she'd *really* like to, if only circumstances had been permitting. *If only we didn't have anxious dogs,* is what she meant. It was my first inculcation into one of the world's great truths: that everything in life is a tradeoff.

Probably just about everybody has some idea of a Dream Room that they'd like to live in someday—and a few lucky people even get the chance to see that dream become a reality. Sometimes, when watching some Netflix show about people building their dream home in,

Spray Anything

say, an abandoned grain silo or former nuclear bunker, I'll admit that I've wept unabashedly at seeing those lucky, lucky people at the end of the hour, now in glorious possession of a sun-soaked home library in what used to be a medieval bell tower, or an immaculately appointed living room sprawling across a space once occupied by a 1920s fire station.

My own conception of the Dream Room I aspire to live in will vary depending upon my mood or state of mind. When feeling particularly stressed out, I'll imagine the sort of Mediterranean living room you see in pictures of Greece—all white walls, white upholstery, tons of sunlight, and the occasional "pop" of aquamarine blue in a throw pillow or wall hanging. In the depths of winter, I'm apt to imagine a sort of English Library living room, with low beamed ceilings, oaken bookcases, well-worn Oriental rugs, comfortable furniture in muted earth tones, and an old stone hearth. If I'm feeling homesick for Miami, the Dream Room I imagine has Spanish influences in its tall windows, high dark-wood ceilings, golden stucco walls, and jewel-tone upholstery.

I've never lived in a room remotely like any of these, and at a certain point in life—and deep into one's forties is probably as good a time as any—I've had to acknowledge that I probably never will. My daydreams may conjure gilded palaces in the air, but my real life is less a showcase for Nice Things and is instead rather more sensibly accessorized by sturdy, sensible, mid-priced furniture—the kind that looks nice *enough*, particularly when accented by cute little throw pillows and suchlike, but that's also designed to withstand years of abuse (or love, depending upon your perspective) without showing too much wear and tear.

Some of this is the result of the inexorable realities of money and circumstances. (It seems to me, for example, the I can live in the Northeast, and I can live in a Greek-influenced Mediterranean-style home, but very likely I can't do both of these things at the same time.) But primarily it comes down to certain choices I've made over the years—choices that I have absolutely zero regrets over, but which, despite my satisfaction with them, inevitably come with consequences.

I'm referring, of course, to the choice I made some twenty-five years ago to become a "cat mom."

I can already hear the protests exclaiming that there are any number of alternatives and solutions available to someone who's determined to make a happy home with both cats on the one hand and furnishings swathed in silks, suede, and antique wood on the other. Frequent claw trimmings, Soft Paws gel caps, ubiquitous scratching posts (which, it's worth noting, are present in abundance in my home), and so on. I've read all the same articles and blogs and expert commentary that everybody else has read, and have followed all the advice that's seemed practicable over the years. But things in life aren't always as straightforward as they're made to seem in self-help guides and advice columns. (This, by the way, is another one of the world's great truths.)

Homer, for example, always had a morbid fear of having his claws trimmed, which intensified, rather than diminishing, over the years. By the time he'd turned ten, you were pretty much taking your life in your hands if you so much as brushed one of Homer's talons with your finger, much less attempted to trim it—a precept that applied not just to hapless groomers and vet techs, but even to me, the person he trusted most. I always understood, though, that the world is an uncertain and often dangerous-seeming place to a little blind cat; if Homer felt safer moving through life secure in the knowledge that he had ten tiny switchblades attached to the ends of his paws, who was I to take that away from him?

Spray Anything

But Homer's claws were far more to him than just his primary weapons of defense or offense. In encountering some new object, for example, whose height Homer was unsure of, he was more apt—at least at first—to attempt scaling it rather than leaping to the top of it, in which case his claws were less like tiny switchblades and more like little pickaxes that helped him scale even the most intimidating of heights. It sometimes seemed to me that Homer's claws were, to him, what my driver's license had been to me when I turned sixteen—something that ensured him both independence and mobility, the freedom to go wherever his fancy might take him. To shear Homer's claws would, therefore, be to rob him of some portion of that spirited independence, which he so fiercely loved and which I so fiercely loved him for.

And it would hardly be reasonable to my other two cats to keep *their* claws trimmed down while allowing Homer's to sharpen until they were practically hypodermic needles—particularly as everybody got older and crankier and more apt to swipe at each other in irritation from time to time. Allowing Homer to refine his claws into razor-sharp points on our various scratching posts while blunting Vashti's and Scarlett's with claw-trimmers would have been tantamount to creating a one-sided arms race in my home—one that would have left Vashti and Scarlett virtually defenseless. It would have upset the entire balance of power—and, as anybody with multiple cats knows, a peaceful group dynamic is a hard-won thing, and one that shouldn't be tampered with.

But, naturally, it wasn't primarily upon each other that my cats exercised their claws. Furniture and human skin bore the brunt of it. I told myself, as I bade tearful farewells to things over the years—to a red velvet loveseat I'd picked up for a song at a moving sale, and that I'd loved with an unreasonable love; to the leather recliner that Laurence had been living with for more than a decade when the four of us moved in with him, and which lasted exactly six months, once subjected to Vashti's tender mercies, before one side of it was stripped all the way down to its wooden frame—that I'd rather have one Homer and one Vashti than a thousand velvet loveseats and leather chairs. There was a life of having Nice Things on the one hand, and then there was having the Good Things in life, which were infinitely more important, on the other—Good Things like love and laughter and the daily miracle of a warm, fuzzy (and, in the case of *my* cats, heavily armed) little critter trusting you enough to fall asleep peacefully on your lap.

There was no question on which side of the equation I placed the cats I loved.

And what did it matter if it was occasionally my skin that got the worst of it? What did it signify if every spirited game of "wiggling fingers under the bedsheets" was apt to leave a days-long reminder of long red welts on the backs of my hands, or if I sometimes—after the brutal slog of bundling Homer into his carrier for a vet's visit—had to slather my wrists in honey for a week in order to speed up the healing process? After all, as my mother reminded me all those years ago, skin does eventually grow back.

That was back in the old days, but even today, things aren't much different. My cat Fanny, ballerina that she is, will leap nimbly from the floor to the top of the mantelpiece, and from the mantelpiece to the top of a seven-foot bookcase, with graceful ease. My three-legged Clayton, however, bless his furry little heart, isn't much of a jumper—which is only to be expected of a cat who has only one hind leg. Clayton works frantically to keep up with his beloved Fanny, and while he doesn't quite succeed in going *everywhere* that Fanny can get to, his ability to climb gets him a good part of the way—and, naturally, climbing requires claws. Nothing breaks my heart more than to see Clayton, fresh from a claw-trimming, trying desperately to huff and puff his way up the side of the couch or the bed, only to fall off helplessly and land on his back, his three legs and pudgy little tummy splayed upward as he turns upon me a look of bewildered betrayal. *Why? Why did you do this to me?!*

(As a side note, it always mystifies me as to *how* it is that Clayton and Fanny can be litter-mates—who eat the exact same food in the exact same quantities every single day—and yet Fanny is slender as a gymnast while Clayton is a mushy little pudge-boy. Genetics are a wacky thing.)

And so, once again, when selecting a new couch for our new home a few months ago, I opted for a sofa swathed in an inexpensive-yet-sturdy gray material that seemed unlikely to show much in the way of claw marks—at least not for the first few years. And, this time around, we opted for a modestly priced metal coffee table to accompany it. We have a small, wooden magazine rack next to the couch, but we mostly keep our magazines in less convenient, tougher-to-get-to spots up out of the cats' reach—Clayton being inordinately fond of shredding anything paper. There's very little more frustrating than coming to the end of one of those looooooooong, four-thousand-word *New Yorker* articles, only to find that a furry miscreant has beaten you to the punch and made confetti out of the last few paragraphs. Hardcover books with paper dustjackets live on the very top shelves of our bookcase, where Clayton can't reach at all and where even Fanny would find it difficult to exercise her scratching impulses without some sort of assistance. We have enough cat scratchers, scratching posts, claw-able cat beds, and sisal-roped climbing cat towers in our house for ten felines or more, but still—there's no point in placing unnecessary temptation in our cats' paths.

Fanny and Clayton are, like most felines, just as engaged by games like "wiggling fingers under the bedsheets" or "catch mom's ankles as she walks by" as my first generation of cats were. Clayton particularly likes to blissfully knead his claws into my stomach, or dig them firmly into the skin of my arms (so as to hug me close) as he lies contentedly on my lap. In the winter months, when my skin is paler, the daily evidence of my cats' love for me on my hands, ankles, and torso is particularly striking (although, fortunately for me, these cats are FAR easier to wrangle into their carriers than my first three cats were).

Sometimes, my cats will love me hardest just before I'm scheduled to do a reading and book signing—and, when someone is standing one foot away from you while you sign a book for them, your scratched and scabby signing hand is about as conspicuous as it's ever going to be. This always provoke a certain amount of consternation in me, as I diligently apply healing balms and unguents to various exposed parts of my body, not wanting to appear unsightly to people who've paid me the incredible honor of traveling to a shelter or bookstore just to meet me.

Occasionally I wonder, though, why I worry about it so much. What, after all, could a few stray claw marks on the person of a well-known cat writer be, if not badges of authenticity?

I VISITED A NEW JERSEY no-kill cat shelter a while back to do a reading, arriving an hour before the reading was scheduled so that a veteran staffer could give me a tour and introduce me to some of the kitties. She was wearing a long-sleeved tee and had pushed the sleeves up to her elbow, revealing forearms that were literally battle-scarred—a veritable topographical map of long white lines that had accrued over more than a decade of being a dedicated cat rescuer. Most of the claw marks and scars were long-since healed, and they crisscrossed her arms from the backs of her hands all the way up to her elbows with reminders of yesteryear's rescue cats.

    I've visited hundreds of shelters over the past decade, and I've met thousands of rescuers. But I couldn't remember ever having seen one who carried such clear visual evidence of her calling—who'd endured more for the sake of spaying and neutering ferals, or patiently helping an anxious cat adjust to life in a shelter environment. They were the arms of someone who refused to give up on any cat, even when those cats did their worst. And I could tell, by the enthusiastic greetings she got from nearly every cat in all of the cage-free "kitty dormitories" we visited, that her persistence had paid off. As a particularly affectionate ginger leapt into her arms by way of greeting, I couldn't help gesturing to her arms and noting, "I guess they're not always this friendly at first." But she just beamed at me and said, "Some of these are love marks, too."

    "Don't let them love you to death," I said wryly, and the staffer laughed cheerfully in response—acknowledging another of the world's great truths: that if love sometimes makes us do strange things, it just as often shows itself in strange ways.

    Back when I lived in Miami, my then-boyfriend Jorge's mother, Maggie, fed a colony of feral cats that lived in the woods near her home. Most of the cats were so shy that they'd duck back into the trees if they so much as caught a glimpse of you, but there was among them an enormous and friendly tom who Jorge's mother had named Pinto.

    Pinto was a stocky gray tabby who Maggie had had neutered, and he was skittish as a wild animal for the first few months after returning to his colony. Over time, however—and after a months-long course of steady feedings accompanied by no loud noises or sudden movements—he became bolder and friendlier. We soon discovered that—for as large as he was and as fierce as he looked (particularly with his one lopped ear)—Pinto was nothing more than a big old lap cat, although he only ever warmed to Maggie and to me. When Jorge and I visited his parents' home on weekends for Sunday brunch, I would spend long hours sitting cross-legged on the ground of their front porch with Pinto's bulk flopped across my lap, purring like a racecar engine as I scratched his back and stroked his head and rubbed beneath his chin while his eyes closed in ecstasy.

Inevitably, of course—and usually long before he was ready—I would eventually have to dislodge Pinto and head back inside. I know that Jorge's parents had a made a brief, abortive attempt at converting Pinto into a house cat, but the experience of bringing Pinto inside had been traumatic enough for all concerned that it wasn't attempted again until an approaching hurricane some months later forced the matter.

But, at that time, going inside meant leaving Pinto behind—something that didn't please Pinto at all. In an effort to stop me, he would rear up and grab at my arms and legs with his claws extended, ruthlessly digging all of those claws into me in an attempt to hold onto me and force me to remain outside with him. And, so, my love sessions with this giant feral kitty who had an even bigger heart—whose manners were, perhaps, not all that they should have been (and what else could you fairly expect from a semi-wild cat?)—would almost always end with a bloody scratch-mark or two. That Pinto loved me, I never doubted. Perhaps he didn't quite love me to death, but he certainly wasn't shy about leaving evidence of his love behind.

I thought about Pinto just the other day while attempting, once again, to pet Oliver on the front steps of my house. As per usual, I came back into the house scratched and bloodied for my troubles. But this time

Spray Anything

Oliver hadn't scratched me while I was petting him. This time, like Pinto, he didn't scratch me at all until I *stopped* petting him and prepared to head inside, when he reared up on his hind legs and wrapped himself around me with all his might, refusing to let me go.

Furtively sneaking into the house and up to the bathroom medicine chest—with its bandages and Neosporin—before Laurence could notice me, I couldn't help but smile and feel pleased as I tended to this latest round of claw-inflicted wounds.

Oliver and I were definitely making progress.

Gwen Cooper

Homer - 2009

The Bells

BY THE TIME I ADOPTED Fanny and Clayton, it had been nearly fifteen years since I'd lived with a kitten. And although my little feline family had felt complete—more than complete—once I'd adopted Homer all those years ago, there had always been a part of me that had longed for the tiny, adorable, curious and obstinate, rough-and-tumble sweetness of a kitten. Since *Homer's Odyssey* had been published a few years earlier, I'd visited more cat shelters in far-flung corners of the country than I could count—and, always, there were kittens in need of homes who I'd cradled and cuddled close and sighed over, before reluctantly returning them back to their caretakers. Fortunately, I'd never followed through on the mad impulse I occasionally felt to simply stuff a kitten into my handbag and stroll out nonchalantly. (*My purse isn't meowing! Maybe* your *purse is meowing!*) But the temptation was a sore one, and Laurence always heaved a barely concealed sigh of relief each time I returned from a shelter visit in possession of no larger number of cats than I'd left home with.

Nevertheless, when Homer suddenly found himself an only cat after the passing of Scarlett—a distinction he'd never wanted and clearly was not enjoying—my first thought had been to adopt some nice, mellow, middle-aged cat as a companion for him. Homer was fifteen by then, after all. A rambunctious kitten would almost certainly require more energy on Homer's part than he seemed able to spare these days.

Homer's obvious grief after we lost Scarlett—the way he dragged himself, like an old man with stiff joints, through our home; the listless manner in which he gave some favored toy a cursory bat with his paw before slinking disconsolately away from it—had been difficult to see, and his sadness had deepened and extended my own. Even four months later, it was impossible to be happy when Homer was unhappy, to feel that I was moving past my grief when Homer so clearly was unable to move past his. Laurence, on more than one occasion, observed that, "This has become a sad house," and he spoke the truth.

And, while it arguably shouldn't have mattered, Homer's grief was made all the more difficult for me to bear by my rock-solid certainty that Scarlett herself—had she wound up as the last cat standing rather than Homer—would have greeted the return of her "only child" status, after so many years of sharing her home with two other cats she'd never wanted, with unabashed glee. *Don't be sad for Scarlett,* I wanted to yell at Homer sometimes. *She wouldn't have been sad for you!* But grief, like all emotions, rarely obeys strict logic, and that sort of reasoning—born as much from my own fear for Homer's health and wellbeing as anything else—almost certainly wouldn't have mattered much to a human mourner, much less a feline one.

Vashti and Scarlett may have gone far out of their way to exclude and avoid Homer as much as possible back in the old days, but they'd nevertheless formed a crucial component of his daily social life. With a seemingly deliberate obliviousness, he had pursued the two of them—trying to engage them in play or long, companionable naps together—every day for fifteen years. Now there was nobody for Homer to play or socialize with, except for a mom who'd never be as good at doing cat things as that cattiest of all possible cats, my Scarlett, had been.

I wasn't sure how Homer would react to having to get used to a new cat for the very first time in his life. Homer, himself, had been my last "new cat." But, after four months of unsuccessful attempts to get Homer out of his funk and coax him back into the spirited playfulness that had once been his trademark, I was both desperate and fresh out of other ideas.

Neither of the mellow, middle-aged cats I'd agreed to foster, however, in the hopes of finding a new companion for Homer, had proved to be a match personality-wise. They'd gone on to forever homes of their own, and in their wake I was left with the growing realization that a kitten, despite my reservations, was probably the best way to go. I was extraordinarily reluctant to add even an additional particle of unhappiness to Homer's already too-heavy burden by forcing upon him the necessity of adjusting himself to a new cat's quirks, preferences, or temperament. A kitten, on the other hand, would be the one to adjust to Homer's personality and preferences—Homer would be the reigning "big cat" of our home—without expecting any similar effort on Homer's part.

It also stood to reason that, if I were going to adopt *one* kitten to be a companion to Homer, then in reality I'd have to adopt *two*—so they could bounce and bandy and tear around our home with each other, hopefully without pestering Homer too much if his own enthusiasm was more limited than theirs.

And so it was that, after fifteen kitten-free years—during which I'd never entirely gotten over my desire to add a new kitten to our household—I suddenly found myself preparing to adopt not just one, but two new kittens at the same time.

SO EXCITED AND RESTLESS WAS I the night before I was due to receive these kittens who were destined (I hoped!) to save Homer from his overwhelming sorrow—so eager with anticipation during the long train ride from Manhattan down to Trenton, NJ, where I was to collect them from a rescue group called Furrever Friends—and so thoroughly prepared was I to adore them, there was probably very little they could have done to disappoint me. Their very kitten-ness was all I asked for at that point, knowing full well that their actual personalities would ultimately be something of a crap shoot. Even if they turned out to be withdrawn or aloof kittens—like Scarlett herself had been—who shunned Homer, I told myself that simply being able to hear them frolicking about in our home, the return of life and activity to what had become a deathly silent apartment, would surely do Homer some good.

Nevertheless, Clayton and Fanny managed to wildly exceed these very modest expectations.

Even with all of a mom's prejudice, I would never suggest that Clayton and Fanny were perfect cats. (Nor would I want them to be—as any cat lover knows, our cats' imperfections are what make them so very loveable.) But the trait that made them perfect for us—the perfect kittens, or so I thought initially, to bring Homer back to himself—was on full display from that very first day when they came to live with us at just under twelve weeks of age.

Whatever their faults and foibles may be, Fanny and Clayton are cats who were very clearly made for love. Without question, they're two of the most physically affectionate cats I've ever seen. Clayton warms to new people instantly, while Fanny, being shyer, takes a bit longer to feel comfortable around newcomers. But they both seem pre-programmed to like or love everybody they meet, and they express their likings in the most demonstrative ways possible—with head bonks, lap jumps, intense cuddling sessions played out to the accompaniment of diesel-engine purrs. They groom each other to a high gloss every day and attempt to do the same for Laurence and me—the loving care expressed by the ritual of it seeming to compel them to keep going regardless of the fact that Laurence and I, despite our cats' best efforts, are unable to achieve anything like their level of shiny sleekness without the application of copious quantities of human-grade grooming products. If we're walking through the house, it's usually with at least one cat rubbing lovingly against our ankles, and rarely do we sit down on the couch or in a desk chair without one or the other of them immediately leaping onto our legs to join us. If we're busy or otherwise not well situated for lap time, then Clayton and Fanny are almost certain to be found curled up with each other, unable to resist the constant impulse to "love on" someone or something else, even in their sleep. When visitors spend the night in our guest room, they're never permitted to spend the night alone, nor even to engage in bedtime preparations without at least one of our cats keeping them company to make sure they aren't lonesome. (Fanny is particularly fond of sitting raptly at the feet of female guests while they perform complicated nighttime beauty rituals.)

    It was obvious that the two of them had been very well loved by the foster mom who'd had them for the first three months of their life; they could never have been so outgoing and confident in their displays of affection if they hadn't come to believe that their little demonstrations would be reciprocated. Their intense love for each other was equally obvious—and it must have seemed to them as natural as breathing to extend their small circle of two wide enough to include others as well.

Of course Clayton and Fanny were fascinated by Homer—always on the smaller side by adult-cat standards, but still the biggest cat our two new kittens had ever seen—right from the start. With eager affection—and within 24 hours of having been released from our guest bedroom for the first time—the kittens progressed almost immediately from following Homer around in silent, respectful enthrallment to trying to include him in their playtimes and grooming sessions and catnap cuddle piles. They batted their toys at Homer's paws, hoping he might bat the toys back. If they came upon Homer in the act of bathing himself, they crawled eagerly atop him, ready to "help" by applying their own tiny tongues to the task. And the sight of Homer attempting to snooze by himself struck them as a tragedy in need of immediate remedy. *Taking a nap, Homer? Howsabout we all curl up together!*

That Homer might not be receptive to these advances—that he might find them bewildering and off-putting—was something that would never have occurred unaided to Fanny and Clayton (especially Clayton—who, to this day, lives firm in the belief that everybody loves him instantly). It was a lesson that Homer, armed with raised paw and warning hiss, had to teach them almost from scratch.

Poor Homer—not only an old man by this time, but also occasionally a crotchety one—had always been an intensely affectionate cat himself. But that was primarily with people. Homer's sole experience with other cats had been with two older sisters who'd never voluntarily touched him or allowed themselves to be touched by him without his having to chase them down first. No other cat had ever wanted to groom Homer with a gently rasping tongue, or cuddle with him as they slept, or follow Homer from room to room in the hopes that *he* might play with *them*.

In a sense, Clayton and Fanny were perfectly suited to give Homer something he'd never had, but had surely

Spray Anything

always wanted. And yet, after all this time, to suddenly be on the receiving end of *so much* cat-on-cat love was something that Homer had never imagined for himself. It was an unexpected windfall to brighten his golden years, to be sure—but Homer was as unprepared to manage this startling embarrassment of riches as someone living in poverty is to suddenly command millions of dollars, should they happen to buy a winning lottery ticket.

    This unprecedented orgy of attention was bewildering for Homer—a bewilderment compounded by the fact that, being blind, of course he could never *see* the kittens coming. It was inevitably disquieting, for example, for Homer to awaken abruptly from a deep sleep, with no advance warning whatsoever, because a small plastic mouse—which Clayton had dragged over to maul while leaning convivially against the warmth of Homer's flank—had been dumped unceremoniously on his head. (*Wanna chew up this mouse with me, Homer?*) Or to be eating from his food bowl, minding his own business, and suddenly find Fanny's tiny tush, seemingly materializing from out of nowhere, pushed solicitously against his snout. (Fanny's…fanny…is a vivid hot pink that's a tad startling against the jet black of her fur, and she takes great pride in showing it off.)

    Homer's hearing had always been uncannily sharp. But it was still nearly impossible for him to hear the kittens approaching on their velvety-soft kitten paws. Even Clayton's three-legged little hop was essentially inaudible—at least until he'd landed square across Homer's belly (and then—believe me—we heard it!). Homer never knew when the newest affectionate attack would come, and, after only a few days, the wear and tear of having to live in a constant state of anticipation was taking its toll. While it was true that Homer began to seem more active and less depressed than he had been, it was the activity of anxiety that primarily propelled him now—a constant state of high alert as he tried to anticipate when and from what direction the newest onslaught would be launched. I'd have been apt to describe the situation by saying that Homer now slept with one eye open, if only Homer'd had eyes. But, even in sleep—or what was passing for Homer's sleep these days—his ears were always up and alert, and he now reposed in a sort of defensive crouch, rather than curled up in the tight little ball that had always indicated he felt completely comfortable and at ease.

This wasn't the change in Homer that I'd been hoping to affect by bringing Clayton and Fanny into his life. I knew that things would be easier for Homer if only I were able to devise some sort of early-warning system that would give him a heads-up that a kitten was approaching well before that kitten was actually on top of him.

I'm embarrassed to admit that the very obvious solution to this problem took me nearly three days to come up with. It finally hit me at six o'clock in the morning over coffee one sunny Wednesday, and that very afternoon I walked down to our local pet store and came home with two kitten-sized, breakaway belled collars—a blue one for Clayton, and a pink one for Fanny.

CONTRARY TO A COMMONLY HELD belief, writing *Homer's Odyssey* has not made me an expert on cats in general, nor on any cats specifically other than my own—and, even when it comes to my own cats, they still manage to surprise me on occasion.

I actually didn't know Fanny and Clayton very well at that point; we'd barely been living together for a week, after all. Still, I knew enough about cats to surmise that getting my kittens into belled collars would likely be a wee bit more complicated than simply fastening the collars onto them one day and letting everything run smoothly from there.

According to an article that I'd read online, the key was to get the kittens used to the collars over a period of days before I attempted actually putting the collars on them. The first step was to gently lay the collars across the backs of the kittens' necks without trying to fasten them, to get Clayton and Fanny used to the collars' weight and sound. *Seems easy enough,* I thought. *How hard could it be?*

Armed with what seemed like a refreshingly simple-to-execute plan of attack, I headed to the living room, belled collars in hand, and shook them until they rang out with an engaging jingle. "Heyyyyyy, kitties," I called, in the tempting tone I usually used when dispensing treats. "Look what I've got. Look what *I've* got, kitties!"

Three-legged Clayton, never one to resist a summoning, came hippity-hopping over first and gave the collars an amiable sniff, followed a moment later by Fanny. Homer had given up playing with any of his many belled toys after we'd lost Scarlett, but from his spot on the couch across the room, he raised his head with mild interest upon hearing the collars' tinkle. Fanny and Clayton continued to give the collars a good going over with their tiny black noses while I stroked their backs reassuringly.

"Now we're just going to gently lay the collars across you, like so..." I told the kittens in a soothing voice, and very carefully draped the collars along the backs of their necks, making no further attempt to fasten them on.

I hadn't expected Clayton and Fanny to *love* the collars, exactly—or even to tolerate them particularly well at first. But I was still unprepared for the vehemence of their reaction, which swiftly went from an interested, *Hmmmm...what are these belled things?* to, *GOOD GOD—SHE'S PUTTING THOSE BELLED THINGS ON TOP OF US!!!* Their little backs arched and puffed, and—apparently firm in the belief that I had just, inexplicably, attempted to murder them—their seven little paws scuttled for purchase on the slippery hardwood floor before the kittens finally skittered off to plunge themselves safely beneath the bed. Clayton was the first to creep out of hiding about a half-hour later (*I guess you weren't* really *trying to kill me,* his forgiving head-bonk conceded), but I wouldn't see Fanny again for a good five hours.

"What's all *that* about?" Laurence inquired, walking into the living room just in time to see Clayton and Fanny dart past his ankles, by all indications in fear for their very lives.

"I think the new guys might be a *wee* bit skittish," I told him drily.

It wasn't much smoother going over the next few days. Every time I approached the kittens with the collars, they reacted as if they were a couple of teenaged girls in a horror movie and I was a crazed spree killer chasing after them with a butcher knife. This was despite my working fun things like treats, catnip, and even a sprinkling of new toys into the routine as I tried with increasing desperation to get them to—at the very least—accept having the belled collars in the general vicinity of their necks. "It's just a collar, you guys," I'd call after their rapidly retreating backsides—alas, to no avail. "A *collar!* It can't *possibly* hurt you!" And then, once I'd found myself alone again, I'd mutter under my breath, *Aye yi yi...*

As it turned out, it was Homer himself who salvaged the situation. The sounds of something belled ringing out—almost immediately followed by the additional clamor of Clayton and Fanny fleeing in terror—finally piqued Homer's curiosity enough that, for the first time in months, he would creep over from the couch to see what all the fuss was about. The kittens having cleared the scene, I'd then dangle the belled collars in front of Homer for his amusement—they should still serve *some* useful

Spray Anything

purpose, I thought—and he'd bat them around with increasing liveliness as the days went by.

I knew I was making progress when, on the third or fourth day, Clayton dared to peek around the corner from the hallway into the living room long enough to observe Homer playing with one of the belled collars. Anything that Homer was intrigued by was also intriguing to Clayton, and soon enough the two of them were batting one of the collars back and forth between them on the ground—Homer with a wariness that bordered on reluctance at the prospect of engaging directly with one of these new cats, and Clayton with wild enthusiasm that Homer had *finally* consented to play with him, if only a little. Homer would swipe at one of the collars in a languid, almost random fashion, and Clayton's little rump and thick, stocky tail would rise straight up in the air as he scampered from side to side, looking for the exact right angle from which to bat the collar back in Homer's direction. It was almost as if he thought he could inject some of his own excitement for this game into Homer, if only he were excited enough about it.

By the end of a week, even Fanny was getting in on the action, and the kittens were engrossed enough in playing with Homer and one of the belled collars that they now barely noticed when I draped the other one across their necks, each kitten in turn.

It was another week before I was able—very slowly and *veeeeery* cautiously—to fasten around the kittens' necks two collars that had been so greatly loosened, they slipped right off the second a kitten shook their head. Each day I made the collars just a bit tighter with less and less protest from Fanny and Clayton. And—after only two weeks of effort—the collars were on the kittens for good.

FROM THEN ON, AND DESPITE the fact that it was only early May, it was Christmas every day in our home—or, at least, it *sounded* like Christmas every day in our home. A merry, sleigh bell-like jingling rang through our rooms and halls and formed the background accompaniment for just about everything we did. From five-thirty in the morning, when I woke up, until some nineteen hours later, when Laurence went to bed, and then all through the night, the happy, jingle-jangle sound of two intrepid and endlessly active kittens festooned in belled collars pealed out. For the first couple of weeks, until we got accustomed to the sound to not hear it much anymore, it was as if some maddened composer—who'd rigorously confined himself to writing music for a single instrument—had moved in with us. I found myself brushing my teeth in time to the silvery tinkling of the bells, unconsciously punching the keys on my computer to the rhythm of that old "Sleigh Ride" song as I wrote. I'd come upon Laurence in the living room, reading a newspaper and—clearly without realizing he was doing it—slapping his hand rhythmically on the coffee table, and I knew that, somewhere in the back of his mind, he was hearing, *Giddy-up! Giddy-up! Giddy-up, let's go...* Sometimes I'd awaken in the dark from dreams of snow and sleds and, in momentary confusion, wonder why the bedroom air conditioner was running in the winter, or how the hallway—as I wandered toward the bathroom—could possibly be so warm in the depths of December.

The sound of tinkling bells had once been Homer's very favorite sound in the world, and it was something he now heard constantly—so constantly that I think it must have been confusing for him at first. So much ringing in our house! As if all the belled toys in the world had been trucked in just for him! When the relentless chiming of bells had finally become overwhelming to the point that Homer—at long last roused from his grief-inspired

Spray Anything

languor to a near-maddened frenzy of playfulness—leapt upon the source of the ringing, only to find a kitten (and not, say, a toy mouse) squirming beneath him, he seemed perplexed. *Why do you sound like a toy?* the startled look on his face telegraphed, before he angrily slapped at whichever kitten it was who'd "fooled" him into getting up from his slumbering position on the couch, and all for nothing.

In short order, however, Homer learned that the silvery sound of a tiny bell ringing was likeliest to mean that Clayton or Fanny, and not some new toy, was approaching. Which isn't to say that he entirely gave up the idea that anything with a tinkling bell attached was a plaything just for him. Although he did come to understand that the belled collars were *attached* to the kittens, he seemed unwilling to accept the idea that they were *for* the kittens. Apparently believing that the kittens had somehow commandeered a ringing toy that was in fact meant for him, he'd do his darnedest to get it "back"—and Clayton was the most frequent target of his raids.

Fanny wasn't afraid of Homer, exactly—she made, for example, a regular habit of sleeping near him on the couch whenever she was ready to settle in for a nice long nap. But Fanny was a shy little girl, and more respectful by nature than Clayton was. After the first few times Homer had greeted her hesitant overtures toward friendliness with an admonishing paw slap, she'd learned to let Homer himself choose the times and manners in which they might play together—and to give him a wide berth the rest of the time.

Clayton, on the other hand, was as persistent in his pursuit of Homer as Homer had once been in his pursuit of Scarlett, no matter how many times Homer delivered a warning paw slap. *Hey—quit it!* Actually, Clayton was more persistent. He followed Homer absolutely everywhere—if Homer loped down the hallway, then

Clayton hippity-hopped after him as fast as his three legs could carry him. If Homer batted a ball of paper across the room, Clayton would eagerly bat it back in Homer's direction—which would only confuse Homer's finely honed sense, perfected by a blind cat over a period of years, as to the exact trajectory a paper ball slapped by him would take. Clayton's interference caused Homer to "lose" his toys more often than not, whereas Clayton couldn't have been more pleased with himself—or more bewildered when Homer would wander off after only one or two back-and-forth volleys. *Look, Homer! I'm playing the same game you are! Hey—where are you going?!!?* If Homer so much as went to use the litter box, Clayton would be waiting impatiently for him just outside. *Whatcha doing in there, Homer? Do you think you'll want to play some more when you're finished?*

No matter how many times Homer slapped or snarled at Clayton, Clayton refused to accept that Homer wasn't as fascinated by him as he was by Homer. Clayton was very far from being the first to wonder how it could be possible to be so obsessed with someone that your entire day revolved around whatever he might be doing at any given moment—and yet, somehow, that someone barely seemed to know or care that you were alive.

As the days went by, however, Homer did begin to show some interest in Clayton—or, rather, in that belled collar that Clayton wore about his neck. Since Homer assumed that the collar was an especially intriguing toy that was his by rights—as all belled toys in our home had always been intended primarily for Homer—he saw no reason why he shouldn't just take it from Clayton. The fact that Clayton was actually *wearing* this particular "toy" was, at most, a minor inconvenience, as far as Homer was concerned.

Accordingly, he would crouch down, poised to spring out at Clayton, whenever he heard the sound of a bell attached to a three-legged kitten approaching, leaping on poor Clayton unawares, pinning him squealing to the ground, and using his teeth to pry the breakaway collar from around Clayton's neck. Then would begin a dedicated game of Keep Away as a somewhat clumsy Clayton—hampered in any game requiring speed by having only three legs—pursued Homer up and down the hallway; up, over, and around the bed; and across counter tops in a fruitless effort to keep up with his fleet-footed idol and snag his collar—that collar he detested wearing in the first place—back from the vise-like grip of Homer's jaw.

That Clayton positively loathed having to wear that collar was abundantly obvious in the unwonted ingenuity he employed in devising ways to get out of it—an ingenuity that was all the more impressive considering how…perhaps the best word is "limited"…Clayton's understanding was in general.

Clayton was the sweetest little kitten imaginable (so mushy, and sooooooo adorable!), but he was very, *very* far from being the brightest cat I'd ever shared my home with. He was, for example, forever plunging his head into boots and sneakers (Clayton being, for unknown reasons, a passionate connoisseur of human foot odor) and then getting it stuck, so that Laurence or I would have to help pull his head out. He was constantly hurling his toys beneath the couch where he couldn't reach them, and then—due to a particularly roly-poly belly—getting trapped at the halfway point as he tried to wriggle under the couch after them, so that Laurence or I would have to grasp Clayton around his midsection and gently tug until he was freed. He was always falling over sideways while trying to scratch behind his ear, chewing on anything wooden (before I learned to hide all wooden objects) until either he cracked a tooth or ended up with a gumful of splinters, crawling into paper bags and then wailing in alarm because—since his hindquarters were facing the bag's entrance—he couldn't figure out how to get back out of the bag. (Thus giving the lie to the very concept of, *the cat's out of the bag!*) For the entire seven years of his existence and to this day, he has remained firmly convinced that the "falling man" in the *Mad Men* opening credits sequence is actually going to fall right on top of him. (*He's coming right at us! RUN FOR IT!!!*)

But the one thing that Clayton was an absolute expert at was divesting himself of his belled collar—and the only thing he hated more than Homer stealing it from him was actually having to wear it. Despite his apparent difficulty in learning in other areas of his life, with astonishing quickness Clayton groked the breakaway nature of the collar, understanding that a certain amount of pressure applied in the correct spot and for long enough would cause it to break apart and fall free of his neck. Even if I cinched the collar on as tightly as it would go without actually threatening Clayton's breathing, he'd manage to patiently work a paw beneath it and then push against the collar until it broke apart, or somehow wedge it on a corner of the coffee table and tug until he broke free of the collar. Sometimes I noted that, if Fanny's teeth landed on the collar during one of their endless mutual-grooming sessions, he'd pull his whole head backward with a sudden jerk, so that Fanny was left with the collar in her mouth while a triumphant Clayton would scoot away, collar- and fancy-free.

Many was the time when Laurence and I would hear the particularly loud jangle of a belled collar as we watched Clayton tearing up the hallway, and then back down, hippity-hopping at top speed back and forth for no apparent reason other than the demands of kitten logic—and then, the fourth or fifth time he came back into view at the end of the hallway closest to the living room, his approach would be silent—the belled collar lying

Spray Anything

abandoned on the floor at the far end of the hallway. Clayton seemed happy enough to forget its existence unless Homer happened upon it a few minutes later—gleefully tossing it up and down in his mouth a few times, just to hear it jingle—at which point Clayton, full of righteous indignation, would chase after Homer, squeaking furiously at his big brother and demanding its return.

I spent an inordinate amount of each day reattaching Clayton's collar around his reluctant neck, while he looked up at me with unhappy eyes that eloquently asked, *Geez, mom...do I have to wear it?* But to see Homer up and playing and running around just like his good old self—the way he'd been only a few months ago, before we'd lost Scarlett—made the effort worthwhile. And Homer—who now spent a not-insignificant portion of his own day stalking the sound of ringing bells through our home, a miniature panther in an urban savannah tracking his prey—seemed to be of the same opinion.

The whole point of the belled collars had been to create opportunities for Homer to play with the kittens if and when he wanted to—or to ignore them altogether, if that was his preference—without having to spend his time dreading that a kitten might be about to sneak up on him or catch him unawares by landing atop him with a wild leap while he was doing something else.

What I hadn't anticipated was that the bells themselves would be what brought Homer back to us.

In our moments of greatest sorrow, we all have an idea of the things that might lift our spirits, if only a little—an old movie, perhaps, or a spontaneous shopping expedition, or some favorite childhood food that only your grandmother knew how to make just the way you liked it. (My own grandmother was, to my knowledge, the only living human being who knew just the right amount of sugar to add to a bowlful of chopped banana and sour cream to make it absolute perfection.) The idea of "comfort food" can be extended to include any number of sights, tastes, and smells. And, for a blind cat, "comfort food" could, of course, be a sound as well. Homer's favorite stuffed worm—the beloved, if inanimate, best friend of his earliest kitten-hood—had had a little silver bell attached to its tail. So had all of the toys Homer had loved when he was young. And the sound of a bell ringing in another room had always meant, to Homer, that one of his much-loved older sisters was playing with something—that maybe if he ran in quickly enough, and tried enthusiastically enough, *this* time would be the time when one or the other of them would finally include him in their games.

The only true misfortune in Homer's life wasn't his blindness, which at any rate never struck him as being nearly as important as it seemed to those around him. It was that a cat as filled with love as Homer was had, through a quirk of fate, wound up with two older sisters who probably did love him—grudgingly, in their own way—but who never felt the need to demonstrate that love in any of the tactile ways (grooming, cuddling, affectionate tail brushes in passing) that would have meant the world to a blind cat for whom touch, in the absence of sight, took on even greater significance.

And now, at the very end of his life, Homer found himself veritably surrounded by love—by two little kittens who were wildly, goofily, insanely in love with him. Kittens who—if only given the chance, if Homer would just let them get close enough—would never get tired of showing him just how much they adored him. The sound of bells ringing in our home no longer just represented an interesting toy, or cats playing at a distance who might or might not let Homer play with them for a moment or two. A bell ringing now meant the approach of a kitten willing to lick Homer's muzzle, to curl up for warmth against his

Spray Anything

belly on the couch, to play any game Homer might feel like playing for however long Homer felt like playing it, on the sole condition that he would let them join in.

As for me, among my own favorite sights and sounds had always been those of Homer racing around our home, busy at his "job" of playing and running and just generally being a happy cat. Whenever I heard the sound of a belled kitten whooshing by, I knew that, coming right after it, would be the sound of Homer—high-spirited and himself once again—chasing after. I would reflect sometimes on the miracle of it—that Homer, so late in life, would finally find so much of the love he must have thought he'd lost with Scarlett not only returned to him, but returned to him tenfold. If Clayton and Fanny have grown up a little spoiled—perhaps just a *tiny* bit overindulged and doted upon—it's only because, to this day, I can't love them or thank them enough for ensuring that my last memories of Homer are as filled with joy and laughter as my earliest ones are.

I'd thought at first that constantly hearing ringing bells in our home—from morning until night, in the background of every single thing Laurence and I did or said—might drive me a little crazy. Eventually, though, it wasn't just that I got used to it. The sound of bells ringing meant that my little feline family was happy and, once again, complete. Very often, as I wrote or showered or did a spot of housecleaning, I'd catch myself, without realizing it, singing under my breath: *Just hear those sleigh bells jingling, ring-ting-tingling too...*

WE MOVED TO A NEW home recently, and in the process of packing up our old place I came across any number of things I'd forgotten about that had found their way, over the years, to the bottoms of drawers and untouched closet corners —newspaper clippings containing reviews of my very first book, published way back in 2007; photos of a much-younger me with old friends, taken on Miami Beach's Lincoln Road in bars and restaurants that no longer existed; a diary I'd kept when I was in the third grade, given to me by my grandmother as a Hanukkah gift.

And, buried way back on a top closet shelf, in a small wooden box containing a clipping of Homer's fur and a little plaster imprint of his paw, I found the small pink and blue collars I'd bought for Fanny and Clayton all those years ago. Clayton's blue collar bore the battle scars inflicted by his claws and Homer's teeth, but otherwise they were still in perfect condition—and still jingled out merrily enough when I gave them a shake.

I was unprepared for the flood of memories that hit me—memories of two intrepid kittens, now middle-aged cats, gamboling through the hallways of our old home. Of Homer, who'd been near-catatonic with grief for so many months, chasing playfully after them. Of how welcome the sounds of life and love had been in our apartment after weeks and weeks of sad, relentless silence. And of how quiet it had seemed once again, after Homer went to sleep for the last time, and we'd finally taken belled collars off the kittens for good.

Fanny and Clayton, drawn by the sound of bells, came upstairs to see what I was up to and found me sitting on the closet floor with the belled collars in my hand. I wondered if they remembered these collars, if hearing them brought back any memories of their youth and of Homer. If Homer could somehow be reconstituted and were to materialize now, here, in front of us, would they recognize him? Would they greet him with the same delight that I would greet the old friends in the pictures I'd found, if we ran into each other again? (*It's so great to see you! How many years has it been?!*) Or would Clayton and Fanny look at him blankly, having lost all trace of even the memory of the big brother they'd idolized once upon a time—when they were so tiny that even a small cat like Homer had towered over their lives and imaginations like a colossus.

Fanny gave the collars a cursory sniff and then, bored, wandered off. But Clayton very carefully grasped the battered blue collar in his teeth. Tugging gently, he drew it from my hand and then scurried off with it, the jingling sound of a little silver bell trailing after him through the hallway and down the stairs.

I let him take it, telling myself that I'd find it again before moving day. And I did look for it later. I checked under beds and tables and the sofa, and even behind the refrigerator. I checked high shelves and low corners. *Where could it be?* I asked Laurence in frustration. *Where could he possibly have hidden it?*

Maybe Clayton buried it in the couch we ended up getting rid of before we moved. Maybe he dropped it into one of the innumerable bags of trash and discarded things we threw away before the moving van came. Maybe he lodged it, unnoticed, beneath an old floorboard or some loosened corner of the carpeting.

Maybe it's simply enough to know that not all mysteries in this life have answers.

In any case, moving day came and went, but I never saw the little blue, belled collar again.

Gwen Cooper

CURL UP WITH A CAT TALE!

Thanks for reading these "tails," collected from the *Curl Up with a Cat Tale* monthly series. If you'd like to enjoy a new cat tale just like these each and every month, go to www.gwencooper.com/cat-tales. Subscribing is inexpensive, super simple, and will give you a fresh dose of feline goodness to look forward to every four weeks! www.gwencooper.com/cat-tales.

For a FREE copy of an exclusive, all-new short story about GwenCooper, visit www.gwencooper.com.

Credit: Robert Calderone

ABOUT THE AUTHOR

Gwen Cooper is the New York Times bestselling author of the memoirs Homer's Odyssey: A Fearless Feline Tale, or How I Learned About Love and Life with a Blind Wonder Cat, Homer: The Ninth Life of a Blind Wonder Cat, and My Life in a Cat House: True Tales of Love, Laughter, and Living with Five Felines, as well as the novel Love Saves the Day, narrated from a rescue cat's point of view. She is a frequent speaker at shelter fundraisers, donates 10% of her royalties from Homer's Odyssey to organizations that serve abused, abandoned, and disabled animals, and has raised over $600,000 for rescue organizations worldwide. Gwen lives in New Jersey with her husband, Laurence. She also lives with her two perfect cats--Clayton "the Tripod" and his litter-mate, Fanny--who aren't impressed with any of it.